Growing in Christ

... from the ground up.

PAULINE HYLTON

CROSSRIVER

ST. JOSEPH, MO USA

To my mother, Pauline Wert.
Your faithful love was an example to
your children and grandchildren.
Your life made a difference not only in our lives,
but in the lives of many others.

Contents

Introduction

"Nothing is going to grow in this red clay. What have we done?" I looked up at my friend Miriam who could tell I was ready to cry. I held squash seeds in one hand while I poked them through white plastic in our newly made raised beds.

Five minutes earlier we'd whooped and hollered and even videotaped as Tom drove our tractor across our newly plowed field pulling the green-machine behind it. The machine built raised beds, laid irrigation tape, covered the bed and tape with a light plastic, and secured the plastic by covering the edges with dirt.

The question was, would anything grow? I highly doubted it.

When we'd sold our fishing business and house on a quarter of an acre in sunny Clearwater, Florida, and moved to an abandoned, sixty-six-acre tobacco farm we inherited outside of Mount Airy, North Carolina (AKA Mayberry), the thought that we might fail at farming never crossed my mind.

Until the day I poked the squash seed into the dry, rocky North Carolina clay.

Imagine my surprise when a few days later I looked out the old farmhouse window that overlooks our field and spied a tiny green shoot peeking through the white plastic.

"Tom! Come quick, it's growing, it's growing!"

The screen porch door banged behind us as we flew toward

the field. Reverently, we got to our knees. We bent over like we'd just witnessed a new birth. And in a way, we did. Tiny leaves popped out through the holes in the white plastic.

"It's a miracle, isn't it?"

Tom smiled. "Yep."

We both smiled as we walked back to our house hand in hand.

That day, a passage of scripture kept running through my mind: "Truly, truly, I say to you, unless a grain of wheat falls into the earth and dies, it remains alone; but if it dies, it bears much fruit" (John 12:24).

Since then, a lot of plants have lived and many have died.

I've died, too.

Kind of.

But like that dead little seed that grew, my faith is growing.

And like the sixty "ladies" who are three-year-old hens and our seventy-five teenage chicks who are dependent on us to feed, water, and protect them, there's not a day that goes by that I don't realize my total dependence on God.

Weakness has a way of requiring you to look up. And that's what I've done.

I'd love to share my journey with you as together we can grow in Christ from the ground up. Although you may not have changed careers in your fifties or been a caregiver for a parent, we all have the same struggles on this earth, and maybe you can see yourself in my struggles. So, I've included a Growing in Christ section at the end of each chapter to get you thinking. And maybe we can grow together.

That is my prayer.

Chapter 1

EXCITEMENT

"Let your smile change the world, but don't let the world change your smile." — Connor Franta

CHICKEN PIN-UPS

Tears poured down my cheeks as laughter erupted from my mouth. My stomach shook and so did Tom's.

My husband and I sat perched on our daughter's bed in her grad-school room looking at chicken pictures in a magazine. It wasn't your typical city-girl magazine. We read from *Mother Earth News.*

The cover consisted of chicken "Pin-Up" pictures. Shiny birds posed in various positions to display their brilliant plumage as they looked demurely into the barnyard. But that's not what had us cackling.

"What do your parents think is so funny?" Sarah's friend asked incredulously.

"I'm not sure…" She leaned against the wall and waited for an explanation.

"We…can't…stop…laughing…because, because…" I snorted as we slipped back into our uncontrolled state of hilarity.

Tom continued, "We're reading about a woman who spent

time each day with her chicks in the sunshine…" We looked at each other and burst out laughing. Again.

I sucked in my breath and persevered. "Then she turned them upside down in a cone and slit their throats!"

Our stomachs jiggled hard as I wiped my nose on Tom's shirt. Sarah and her friend made a quick getaway while Tom and I gained our composure. It wasn't the actual demise of the bird that had us cackling; it was the distant thought that we might ever be able to turn a chicken upside down and end its chicken life.

Because at that point in fifty some years, we had decided to change our lives forever and move from our comfortable charter fishing boat business in sunny Clearwater, Florida, to a broken-down, sixty-six-acre tobacco farm in North Carolina.

And I wanted chickens.

And did I mention it was in Mount Airy, North Carolina— AKA Mayberry?

Let me answer a few questions before we go on.

No, we'd never grown anything.

No, we didn't win the lottery.

No, we weren't homeless.

At that point, we didn't think we were crazy. I'm not so sure now.

We were cultivating a dream. Discontented with our home in crowded Pinellas County, Florida, we desired a quieter, simpler life. Pictures of beautiful green pastures filled with contented livestock filled our dreams. Scenes of the two of us walking hand in hand through daisy-covered fields, picking perfect vegetables played non-stop through my head.

We'd thought about the move for three years, but there were other issues to consider before we made this life-altering change (besides the fact that we were well into our fifties)—like my ninety-two-year-old mom who lived in our fourth bedroom.

My parents moved in with us in 2002 when my kids were

teenagers. Dad died in 2007 and Mom depended on us to oversee her care. Could she handle the move?

What about our twenty-one-year-old son? He still lived with us. He worked part-time and attended school part-time. How would the move affect him?

Tom and I prayed and waited and dreamed and prayed. Now that I look back on that time, it's funny how I thought the Lord would answer our prayers. He has answered almost all of them, but not at all like I thought He would.

THE CONFERENCE

A few months later, we decided to attend a sustainable farming conference, so we flew to Winston-Salem, North Carolina, to learn a few things.

"You sit in on the mushroom workshop and I'll go to soil quality," Tom said as we parted ways in the busy hotel lobby. We'd been at the conference for less than twenty-four hours and already our heads were swimming.

"We need worms," Tom stated matter-of-factly as we met up later. "A guy said he's been farming for fifteen years, and his soil isn't where he wants it yet. But worms are where it's at."

Who knew people thought so much about dirt?

"I learned that you can grow mushrooms just about anywhere. Some people grow them in garbage bags and some in wood. Get this! The speaker goes around inoculating tree stumps with mushroom spores, and then collects them after they grow. You'd think there would be a law against that or something." I paused. "He got $200 for one mushroom!"

Tom gawked at me. Mushrooms were definitely on our growing list.

"I also learned about Heritage Breed Chickens verses hybrids." And so our conversation ebbed and flowed while we grabbed food, attended a keynote session, and went to bed with visions of vegetables dancing in our heads.

The next morning, I sat down outside of a workshop next to an attractive young lady while Tom decided to hit a class on livestock production. We began a friendly conversation.

"How are you involved in sustainable farming?" I asked.

"My father and I have about 200 cows that we are about ready to process—that means butcher." She smiled. "We're just trying to figure out how to finish them off."

Shocked, I had thoughts like: Will they do the deed with a candlestick in the library? Or a pistol in the kitchen? Isn't there some cow protection society?

She must have sensed my horror because she said kindly, "Finish them off means what kind of grain to feed them before we send them to market."

We sure had a lot to learn. So, Tom bought every single book the conference sold.

Or at least I thought he did.

AN ANNIVERSARY TRIP

"Have you packed everything in the car? What about the snack cooler?" I asked Tom as I finished brushing my teeth. Over 700 miles was no small trip. We almost always began in the early morning hours. And this was no exception. Our coffee thermos held a full load of strong coffee, a CD suspense novel sat on the front seat of our truck, and our newly purchased farm boots rested on the floorboards.

By four a.m. we were off to celebrate our thirtieth anniversary on the farm.

We arrived close to dinnertime (or supper in the South).

Staying at the old homestead was both an experience and a treat. An experience because we arrived at the 100-year-old home built by Tom's grandfather that usually sat vacant for a year so the bugs took possession in our absence. Entering always involved some fear and trepidation. After the initial entry and the "All Clear" sign from Tom, we'd sweep and clean up. It's amazing how many dead bugs you can fit in a dustpan.

Another experience was going to the bathroom. Although it was attached, it sat outside the main part of the house. Side-stepping spiders on uneven floors while trying to find the bathroom at two a.m. always got my blood boiling.

It wasn't camping, but close.

It was a treat because we took time to eat well and slow down. Grocery shopping appeared next on our list, and in Mount Airy, Lowes Foods offered a wide variety of specialty foods that we looked forward to on our trips. The local meat market carried pasture-raised meat and seafood from the coast. Every night hosted a variety of culinary delights.

We savored the goodness of the local food and the beautiful scenery without being rushed. Each evening we lounged on rocking chairs while listening to our book on CD. Fireflies danced in the moonlight as mosquito candles flickered on the porch railings. We dreamed like the young and talked like teenagers. There were long periods of comfortable silence. Often, Tom opened the Bible and we prayed.

On our actual anniversary, we took Tom's cousin to dinner at a local steak place. I wore black heels that should be illegal for anyone over fifty, and we talked. They spoke of long-ago times when their grandparents were still alive and Tom rode up and visited with his North Carolina family. They reminisced of whole days butchering pigs and canning vegetables.

I wondered what it would have been like living around a

large extended family in a small town. Since my parents were Salvation Army officers, I moved every three to four years and made new friends each time, along with living in a new house. Small town life was new to me and I wondered if I'd like it.

OUR ANNIVERSARY GIFT

"She's a good one," the stout man said in his Southern drawl.

"I've heard that," Tom responded. "I've done quite a bit of research on the Internet, and this Kubota model got great reviews. We thought about buying used, but they're almost as expensive as the new."

The man nodded and leaned lazily against the tractor.

I stared at the giant orange machine. I think it was the first time I'd seen a tractor up close. The wheels came to my chest, and the metal top towered above me.

"Would ya like to take her for a spin?" the salesman asked.

"No!" we shouted in unison. Didn't he know we were city people who had no idea how to operate a tractor? Much less in public where we could actually hurt people!

So, to celebrate thirty years of marriage, while vacationing at the farm, we bought a tractor.

And a front loader. (It's another expensive farm thing.)

The next day, they delivered the tractor with the front loader attached.

The man who delivered the machine dropped it at the end of our driveway.

"Um, could you please pull it off the driveway?" Tom asked.

The driver looked skeptical.

"I've never driven a tractor before," Tom admitted sheepishly.

The driver gawked at him. "Sure thing," he said in his polite Southern accent. Inside, I believe his thoughts had something to do with Yankee and What in tarnation?

After the deliveryman left, we stared at our new purchase like new parents stare at a newborn.

"I guess we should try it out," Tom said.

"You practice and let me know when you've got it, then I'll try it with you." I went inside to start dinner. Every once in a while, I'd spy out the front window of the farmhouse as Tom made crisscross patterns in the field. I couldn't help but smile.

After a while, he motioned for me to join him. I climbed up on the side with the metal step. "Sit here and hold on overhead," Tom stated. "Be sure not to knock this lever, or it may knock it out of gear."

I nodded. And off we drove into the sunset on our orange Kubota with me in my purple and pink Target boots and my hair flying in the wind.

Both of us grinned from ear to ear.

OUR FIRST REAL FARMING

Although we were on vacation, we were anxious to get started on farming. "Do you have any hairy vetch?" I asked the elderly man behind the counter.

His face screwed up and his lips drew back. "Any what?"

"It's a cover crop that puts nitrogen in the soil," Tom explained.

"Never heard of it," he paused and smiled, "but we can try and get it fer ya. My suggestion is to go with winter rye and mix it with clover and oats. And you'll also need lime—lots of it."

After the gentleman at the farm store told us how much to buy, how to spread the seed, took our money—by check no less since they didn't take cards—we drove home with the expectancy of kids on the way out of school for the summer break.

We arrived at the farmhouse with a few hundred pounds of

seed. We'd read about cover crops and even attended seminars about the seed you put down to improve the soil by putting organic matter into it. (You'll hear *organic matter* a lot, especially when I talk about chickens.) Just understand this…organic matter is important. Real important.

Our big red seed spreader attached easily to the orange tractor. "How do we mix the seed?" I asked. It's not like we were mixing a bucket full. We'd purchased three types of seed, and the formula was two parts rye, one part clover, one part oats.

"Let's mix it like cake batter," Tom suggested. It sounded like a great idea. Anything with oats should be stirred. He grabbed a big stick and we poured and mixed and stirred and mixed.

Tom took out the directions to the seed mixer. "It says to go ten mph and open the hole to a five in order to get an even spread."

He mounted our anniversary present. I felt as if I was sending him off to war. "Goodbye, my love, and good luck!" We gave each other the thumbs-up sign and off he drove at ten mph on our rocky, uneven ground.

Right now, if you were a farmer, you'd be rolling on the floor. You see, ten mph is slow for a car but like the Indianapolis 500 for a tractor.

Tom flew through the air, holding on to the steering wheel for dear life. I watched in horror as he bounced, cartoon-like, on our mechanical bucking bronco.

"Please let him live, Lord!" I prayed.

He did. Tom re-evaluated his speed and finished the field. It was enough farming for one day.

OUR NAME AND OUR HOME

As I studied Genesis in Bible Study Fellowship, I came across Genesis 30:37–43:

"Then Jacob took fresh rods of poplar and almond and plane trees, and peeled white stripes in them, exposing the white which was in the rods. He set rods which he had peeled in front of the flocks in the gutters, even in the watering troughs, where the flocks came to drink; and they mated when they came to drink. So the flocks mated by the rods, and the flocks brought forth striped, speckled, and spotted. Jacob separated the lambs, and made the flocks face toward the striped and all the black in the flock of Laban; and he put his own herds apart, and did not put them with Laban's flock. Moreover, whenever the stronger of the flock were mating, Jacob would place the rods in the sight of the flock in the gutters, so that they might mate by the rods; but when the flock was feeble, he did not put them in; so the feebler were Laban's and the stronger Jacob's. So the man became exceedingly prosperous, and had large flocks and female and male servants and camels and donkeys."

He did some ancient shepherding tricks, but he knew God gave the increase. I loved that idea.

On the porch that evening, I brought up the topic of our farm name. "Tom, I think we should name our place Peeled Poplar Farm, after Jacob in the book of Genesis. I believe it teaches that God gives the increase. And Lord knows we're going to need all the help we can get."

We agreed. Peeled Poplar Farm it would be.

But we still needed to choose our home site.

The next day Tom said, "Pauline, get the orange tape and I'll get my measurer. I've also got sticks for us."

Years earlier when the farm still had over one hundred acres, we had hiked through a dense part of the woods and found a flat piece of land. We had already looked at four or five other places to build. I sat on a log and looked up. Bright green trees shown through the underbrush and met a Carolina blue sky. Mesmerized, I lay down and looked up.

"Tom, come over here and look up with me." A soft wind blew leaves in a swaying motion as if dancing to the Creator's tune. "I love this place. Let's live here."

So, on our anniversary trip, we brought the orange tape out and began to measure. Sammy, our Standard Poodle, stayed right by our sides since he was used to walking on a leash in a city. The leaves scared him.

Surprisingly, when we followed a path away from the trees, we came upon a fence and a beautiful pasture with contented cows. It wasn't our property, but what a view!

"Which direction do you want the house to face?"

"South, toward the pasture, of course." We had macheted our way to this part of the property and even down to the neighbor's fence. Because of the dense underbrush, I couldn't see Tom even though he was less than twenty feet away.

"Let's put it a hundred feet from the fence and a hundred feet from the back of the area we would have to have cleared." We'd decided on a little less than two acres for our home site, with a winding driveway through the woods.

It took all day. We could barely see each other from the overgrown trees.

We meandered through trees with our tape, mapping out the drive and putting sticks up on the corners. (You'd be surprised how hard it is to make a straight line when you have no point of reference. And then to have the lines meet almost takes a doctorate plus a lot of luck.)

I couldn't picture what the site would look like without trees and with a house, but our excitement couldn't be squelched.

We headed back to the old farmhouse that would belong to Tom's sister, to clean up, make our feast, and enjoy the porch. It had been a good day.

THE ORCHARD MAN

We hired a man to do the excavation for the house even though he couldn't start until winter. On one of our last days on the farm, we made our last stop. Not only did I want chickens, but an orchard sounded romantic, so, we visited a tree nursery.

The owner stood tall, donning the obligatory farmer overalls. A toothpick rested on one side of his mouth. He surveyed us and smiled, as his toothpick remained steady.

After a few minutes I asked, "How much are your peach trees?"

"Fifteen dollars unless you buy more than twenty-five, then the price drops to twelve."

In my mind, I had pictured us planting a few hundred fruit trees, putting water bags around them while we still lived in Florida, and by the time we moved, we'd have bushels of fruit!

I continued, "So when you plant them, you dig a hole?"

His toothpick wavered. "Yes, ma'am, you dig a hole, a big hole."

"And then you drop the tree in, right?"

He shifted from one boot to the other. "Yes, then you put the tree in the hole." He stared hard at me.

I threw the conversation ball to him, but he wasn't really throwing it back. I fished for more information with the water bag scene in mind. "Then you have to water them, right?"

His toothpick shifted furiously from side to side. "Yes, ma'am, you do have to water them."

By then we knew we weren't ready for an orchard, and this man probably wouldn't sell us any of his trees.

I'd not had much success with live plants. In fact, Tom told any houseplants I'd buy at the store, "You're coming home to die!"

Still, I dreamed of luscious, bug-free orchards at Peeled Poplar Farm. I sure had a lot to learn.

GROWING IN CHRIST

Adventures from the Lord can be exciting! It makes me think about the disciples in Mark 6:6-13:

"Then Jesus went from village to village, teaching the people. And he called his twelve disciples together and began sending them out two by two, giving them authority to cast out evil spirits. He told them to take nothing for their journey except a walking stick—no food, no traveler's bag, no money. He allowed them to wear sandals but not to take a change of clothes.

'Wherever you go,' he said, 'stay in the same house until you leave town. But if any place refuses to welcome you or listen to you, shake its dust from your feet as you leave to show that you have abandoned those people to their fate.'

So the disciples went out, telling everyone they met to repent of their sins and turn to God. And they cast out many demons and healed many sick people, anointing them with olive oil" (NLT).

I can't imagine what it was like to hang around with Jesus for three years. These guys saw miracle after miracle. They sat under His all-wise teaching. They watched Him hug children and raise people from the dead. Now He was commissioning them to spread the good news of the gospel. And on top of that, He gave them authority to cast out demons and heal the sick. They must have been pumped!

We were ecstatic! Often, I'd find myself humming the James Taylor song, "Carolina on my Mind," while I breezed through the day. We couldn't wait to begin this new adventure from the Lord.

I know several young missionaries who cannot wait to go to some unreached people group. Or there are the missionaries who come back to the States on furlough and can't wait to go back to the country where they are serving.

In the next few years we would experience profound difficulties along with deep-filled joy in our new adventure.

What about you? Is there an adventure out there the Lord is prompting you to take?

Enjoy those adventures. Be glad the Lord gives them, and be happy to have the capacity to take them.

Here is what I learned through the excitement.

Don't forget the Lord is with you. He is not bound by space or time or culture. He knows when a sparrow falls and even when you lose a hair. He doesn't just live in big cities or far countries. He is here. And there. Count on that.

Don't forget the Lord. After forty years wandering in the wilderness being totally dependent on Jehovah, the Israelites were about to enter the promised land. Here is what God told them:

"But that is the time to be careful! Beware that in your plenty you do not forget the LORD your God and disobey his commands, regulations, and decrees that I am giving you today. For when you have become full and prosperous and have built fine homes to live in, and when your flocks and herds have become very large and your silver and gold have multiplied along with everything else, be careful! Do not become proud at that time and forget the LORD your God, who rescued you from slavery in the land of Egypt" (Deuteronomy 8:11–14 NLT).

Friend, the Lord brought me out of slavery. If you are His child, He brought you out, too. I'd like to tell you something—just between you and me—sometimes I wander back over enemy lines because I forget about God when things are going well.

Don't lose your excitement, but remember the God who is with you.

Chapter 2

FEAR

"For God has not given us a spirit of fear, but of power and of love and of a sound mind." 2 Timothy 1:7 NKJV

AM I SURE?

Pauline, you know the land is just sitting there?" Tom suggested several months before we committed to the move.

I sipped strong coffee as I sat propped up in bed, enjoying the morning sun filtering through leaves outside our sunny Florida windows.

"So?" I said absently, taking another sip. "I'm just not sure."

He paused. "Why don't you want to sell everything and move there?"

"Because I'm afraid."

"Afraid of what?"

The word barely came out of my mouth. "Everything."

The familiar was comfortable—not perfect, but comfortable. I'd attended a great church for over thirty years, had really good friends and neighbors, and there was a Starbucks within walking distance.

It's not that I didn't love the farm. Each time I visited the homestead, I enjoyed watching cows graze on green hills and horses drift through flowery pastures. But I couldn't wait to get home. Thoughts like, Why would anyone want to live here? I mean, what do people do all day? There is no shopping to speak of, hardly any restaurants, and no beaches. I don't think I could ever live on the farm.

Tom was right, though. The land was sitting there, and did I mention it was free? Plus, Surry County, North Carolina, would be much more affordable than Pinellas County, Florida.

"You know our business gets harder and harder every year. The costs keep going up, and frankly, if there were some kind of recession, our business would sink."

That disturbed me because we owned and operated a charter fishing boat on Clearwater Beach.

"Really think about it, Pauline."

I did. And prayed. And both.

The Lord soothed my heart and warmed my soul. I felt a "nod" from the Holy Spirit that the farm idea stemmed from Him. And His plans are always good. The best, even. And He has the resources to work out His plans for both His pleasure and my good.

And that was my desire. That is my desire. He owns the cattle on a thousand hills, and He was giving us a few of those hills.

The fear never really went away, and frankly, fear will never go away on this earth. But I pushed it aside for the present.

ARE YOU CRAZY?

A few months later, I pulled out the satellite map we'd purchased from the county of our property in North Carolina and spread it across our dining room table.

"This is our property, and this is our neighbor. He has horses and a few of them are on this part of our property." I pointed to a green portion of the map and smiled. "This is where we are going to have our house built and the driveway will run through this section. It looks like it will have to be about 900' long." I pointed to another green portion of the map.

My friend's eyes glazed over. "Are you sure about this, Pauline? I mean, you've lived here a long time and farming is hard work, and you don't really know anyone there."

She had a point. Truth be told, I thought when we moved, I'd be a writer with a garden. Tom would do all the real heavy farm work. But I worried about moving away from my friends and especially my church. My children grew up in that church and I loved the people.

My best friends were supportive, but their idea of roughing it was a three-star hotel. Would anyone come to visit me? I wondered.

Tom came home that night from our charter fishing business. "I had a farmer as a customer on the boat today. He grows wheat in Kansas. I told him we were moving to a farm. He looked at me and said, 'Are you crazy?'"

"Are we?" I wondered out loud.

IT'S TIME

"I guess we're going to be staying in Florida," Tom said one night as we went to bed. Tom had traveled to the property in North Carolina as they cleared our land and constructed our driveway. He videoed the driveway from the truck and showed me around where the land was cleared. We figured we'd just be using the place as a campground since there seemed to be no interest in our charter fishing business.

That's the way it looked to both of us. We had our boat listed. Several people said they were interested, but no one showed us the money. We'd prayed about the move and just figured it wasn't in God's plan.

Until one Saturday.

Tom came home from the dock with a funny look on his face after fishing.

"A man came by the boat today and asked me to take him for a ride tomorrow."

I thought that was weird since it was Sunday, and we almost always took the day off to worship. His next sentence shocked me.

"He said he's interested in buying our boat."

My jaw dropped several times over the next few days since the man wrote us a check for most of the amount by the following Tuesday.

The new owner sat at our dining room table. "So, how long would you like me to stay on?" Tom asked cheerfully.

"That won't be necessary. I've already hired a captain."

Tom and I always thought he'd have a job for a month or two after we sold the boat, for two reasons: our customers loved Tom, and most thought he was the best fisherman in our marina. Naturally, we thought the new owners would like to do a smooth transition by passing the baton with Tom's help.

Wrong again. As we took the check from the new owner, Tom lost his job, and I didn't have one.

It was time to pack.

PACKING FOR CANAAN

Then there was the house issue. In the twelve years we'd owned it, we'd shared it with countless people—a French student, a girl from Uganda, a young man from Pakistan, my parents, many neighbors, and of course loads of people from our church.

The trouble is, when you're busy showing hospitality and

running a business, there's not much time for renovation. Or even maintenance. So, in three weeks we did twelve years of home renewing and renovation. The good thing was that the sixteen-hour days six days a week prepared us for our farm schedule. We just didn't know it yet.

I think my friend Kathy almost *magically erased* my whole house. She reported about every other day around noon and kept me working until eleven p.m.

"Pauline, you have to label the boxes on the top and the side. I'm telling you, I just got through moving, and if you don't, you won't be able to find anything!"

I succumbed to everything she commanded, but I grew wearier by the day. Who knew packing up a four-bedroom, three-bathroom house and putting it on the market could take so much work?

Everyone else in the world, that's who.

While I cleaned and packed, unemployed Tom remodeled two bathrooms, fixed gutters, and repainted everything that looked dingy. Our self-imposed, putting-the-house-on-the-market deadline loomed nearer.

Each night we fell into bed barely recognizing each other our eyes were so bleary.

"It's gonna be fun, right, Tom?"

All I heard was snoring.

WORD GETS OUT

First, we had to tell our kids we'd sold our business and were moving. I use the term "kids" lightly since Sarah was nicely tucked away in Tallahassee with a new husband and a good job. Micah still lived with us but went to community college plus had a job.

Sarah cried while Micah asked, "How much?"

I also had to tell my ninety-two-year-old mom who lived in our fourth bedroom.

I cleared my throat and sat on the edge of her bed while she lounged in her lift chair with a book. She looked up. "Mom, we sold the boat and we're moving to North Carolina!" I blurted out so fast I could have been from New York. "You know we've talked about it for a while, and you'll be moving with us, and we'll have land and chickens and an orchard." I caught my breath. "You'll love it!"

She closed her book and gave me a tired look. "It snows there, doesn't it?"

"No, Mom, it never snows there."

"I'll be cold."

"Mom, we'll build a house and have good heaters, and if you're cold I'll put a heater in your room."

"Are you sure, Pauline?" She gave me that mom-to-daughter-look-eyes and I almost cried.

My lips said, "Yep! I'm so excited! You'll love it, too!" Inside I thought, No, Mom, I'm not sure, but Tom just lost the only job he's ever had and now we're committed.

Over time, we all adjusted to the idea of picking up our roots and moving, but it wasn't as easy as I thought.

GROWING IN CHRIST

I remember as a child sitting on my bed, feet tucked securely under the blankets, sheet wrapped tightly around my neck to prevent the giant, six-foot mouse who lived under my bed from nibbling me to death. I don't know how I came up with such a creature—probably my big sister. Convincing her little sister of a killer rodent was her idea of fun.

Often, the thought of my imaginary monster kept me from

getting up, even to ask for help or comfort.

Fear is like that. It keeps us from a deeper faith. And a lack of faith can keep us from action. Fear almost kept me from farming in the foothills of North Carolina. And you wouldn't be reading this book.

Fear can also keep us from reaching out. One time, I was washing my hands in a public restroom when a woman stood next to me. I felt strongly that I should share the gospel with her. The Holy Spirit was as loud as the suspenseful music you hear in a horror movie just before the killer appears. "Speak to her!" His Spirit said. I continued washing my hands. Inwardly, I said, that is just plain weird, Lord. She might think I'm a creep. Fear kept me at the sink.

And then she walked out the door. I'd missed my chance. Some other servant of God was given the privilege of sharing the gospel.

And when we step out in faith, God rewards us. Once discouragement almost overwhelmed me. I felt as if I was a lousy parent and even a lousier Christian. "Please, Lord, I need some encouragement today. Send someone along with a word from You."

I pulled into the parking lot of a coffee shop to write. Plunking down at a cleared table, I noticed an older man watching me. After a while, we struck up a conversation. We talked about his wife dying, and how he came to the shop each day to get out. I shared with him that I was a Christian writer. After that I shared the gospel with him, beginning with the patriarchs. The more I spoke, the more confident I became. The more encouraged I felt.

After I finished, he stared at me like I had a third eye. "You really believe that?"

"I'm basing my life on it," I said confidently.

Fear shouldn't keep us from faith. All we need is to take a baby step—He does the rest.

Fear is inevitable in this world. But fear shouldn't rule our lives as believers. Scripture says this in Romans 8:28 NLT, "And we know that God causes everything to work together for the good of those who love God and are called according to his purpose for them."

How does that work itself out? Let me give you an example in my life. There is a situation right now that seems hopeless and bound for tragedy. There is absolutely nothing I can do to prevent it. I continually pray for this situation. And I could be so fearful of what and when and how something may happen it would paralyze me.

My thinking goes something like this…I know God is good even when I cannot see it. I know God is sovereign when I do not understand it. I know God is loving when I do not feel it. How? Because God's Word tells me all of the above. When I depend on my feelings, I'm a mess.

What are you afraid of right now? Be honest with yourself. Write it down. Share it with the Lord. He is the Good Shepherd. He knows and He cares.

Chapter 3

CHANGE

My Florida pastor says the only one who likes change is a baby.

TOM'S ABSENCE AND MY VISIT

Tom's sister graciously agreed to rent the farmhouse to us since we'd split the land, and she owned the old homestead. We planned on building a house. But for the present, living close to our land was a plus, so renting the farmhouse worked out great. We knew we would need to make a few changes to accommodate Mom.

The plan was to drive our truck to the farmhouse and do some work. After a few days, I'd fly home while Tom renovated Mom's room. First, we would need to pack up all Tom's mother's belongings from the farmhouse so we could fit ours in. Her furniture would remain, so we would rent a storage unit near the farmhouse for our stuff.

We assumed there would be a lot of bugs at the farmhouse since no one had been there since our visit in October, but we weren't prepared for the infestation. Flies swarmed under the cabinets, spiders crept along the baseboards, and ladybugs coated the kitchen window. As we moved some of the furniture up into the attic, some flies swarmed at me.

Running downstairs, I dashed out the back porch and fell to the grass, sobbing. "I can't take this anymore! There are so many bugs and so much work. How are we going to get everything finished?"

Tom sat beside me. He hated bugs worse than I did. "It'll get better, Pauline."

And it did. As the house got cleaned and we stored some of the stuff, we had time to look around a bit. We even discovered a good Thai restaurant in Mount Airy.

That night on the porch, Tom said, "I want to build a house, Pauline."

"I know, Tom, but we don't have the same amount of time as Noah did. We're moving here in a few weeks and beginning to farm, which by the way we know nothing about."

Now I know Tom would have built the best house in the world, but we didn't have the time or the energy, and we both knew it.

One day, while chatting with the owner of the storage unit in Dobson, we asked him who he recommended to construct our house. We explained our very limited budget.

"If I were you, I'd buy a modular home. They are really well made, as good as stick built." (That means wood.) "The place next door does a great job, and they've been in business for a while."

"Howdy," the owner stated as we entered the office. By the time we walked out, we'd decided on a 26' by 60' model that had a big center room for entertaining, three bedrooms, and two bathrooms. A few days later, we picked the kitchen cabinets, appliance colors, and bathroom floorings. (It helped that we only had three choices.)

"We'll bring you the down payment after we close on our Florida house," Tom said a few days later. Just like that, we bought a house without looking at it and celebrated with burritos at the local Mexican restaurant.

I flew out the next day. I took care of last-minute arrangements at home, while Tom finished up at the farmhouse. Tom flew back about a week before we were scheduled to move.

I couldn't believe it.

SOLD

My friend staged our house, which means we emptied it of everything we owned, stored our stuff except for one chair, and sat on the floor at night until it sold.

It took a week.

It was time for goodbyes.

There were easy goodbyes—the grocer, coffee barista, and mailman. Then some not-so-easy-goodbyes.

The plan was to attend church on April 28, load the rest of our stuff, and leave before dawn on Tuesday, April 30. Our last Sunday came faster than I imagined, and I was down to sing. As I sang Phil Wicham's, "Ceilo," my heart filled with thoughts of heaven and my heavenly family I would leave in a few short days. I looked out over old and new friends, men and women I'd watch grow up and start their own families. Although I knew we were leaving, it seemed surreal.

Three couples came over to join us for dinner our last evening home. We ordered Chinese and ate off paper plates. One would talk about a party we'd had, another spoke of all the fresh fish they'd enjoyed.

"Pauline, remember the first time you had us over for dinner and you handed Josiah the spaghetti on a Styrofoam plate that fell right into his lap?" He snorted.

"Yes, I'm glad he didn't get third degree burns," I recollected.

We laughed, chatted, cried, and prayed. I knew we were life-long friends, but I'd moved enough when I was a kid to know things would never be the same.

We said goodbyes with promises of visits and cards, and then, after years of coming and going at our home, our friends left our house forever.

THE DAY

Our gigantic-sized moving van could only hold so much. The antique dining room set didn't fit, along with a few dressers and various lawn accessories.

"You up, Micah? Remember you're loading Grandma's hospital bed with Dad." Micah pulled the covers off, scrunched his eyes, and searched for his glasses. The plan was to load Mom's stuff and the wheelchair into our van. Mom's caregiver, Paula, would accompany us to our new home in our van and remain for a few weeks to make sure Mom made a smooth transition. Tom and Sam (our Standard Poodle) would follow in the moving van.

Not only were we moving away from our friends and family, we left our son behind. His life as an adult began the moment we pulled out of the driveway.

I grabbed Micah and held him tight. "We love you, son, and we're praying for you." Then I marched out the door. Rain spattered the driveway as we helped Mom into our well-used blue van. We put her in the front seat, while Paula stepped over coolers and clothes to find a small vacancy in the back, wedged tightly between kitchen tools and books.

"And we're off!" I said to Paula and my mom after we pulled out of the driveway for the last time. In the darkness, I passed the Einstein's where I took the kids during our home school outings, the store where I got a morning cup of coffee and my children looked forward to a cookie. We drove past the mall and onto the causeway that separates Clearwater from Tampa.

Warm breezes swayed stately palms as waves lapped the sandy beach. I didn't talk much for the first few hours since I didn't trust my voice to speak, and I kept having to wipe my eyes.

THE ROAD TRIP

"Slow down, Pauline!" Mom reiterated for the hundredth time. Normally she slept about sixteen hours a day, but for our thirteen-hour drive she was full throttle.

"How about we stop at Starbucks and get a coffee?" I suggested. All three of us unloaded at the coffee shop. Mom ambled into the store and gawked at the merchandise. I'd forgotten how little Mom got out. She mostly went to the hairdresser and an occasional Sunday service. Her health had kept her home most of the time.

"I'll order." I came back with the basics and a few sweet things.

"Thank you," she said cheerily. Funny how I never noticed how my mother was so grateful for the least little service. After a while, we loaded into the car with the hope of making it to South Carolina. I thought Mom would go to sleep, but I was wrong. She continued her commentary on my driving as she pointed out various state license plates.

Tom and Sam followed about a half hour behind us, but we decided to meet up for dinner at Cracker Barrel. While Tom made his way to us, Mom sat on the Cracker Barrel porch in a comfy rocking chair for a bit, then the three of us got a table and enjoyed some hot tea. Mom continued to look around at the people and smile.

"This is so nice, Pauline. What a nice dinner," she said when we left. Who knew I'd picked a five-star restaurant, at least by Mom's standards?

At about 7:30 p.m. we exited Highway 77. We traveled the

three miles into a small town, and as we did, we passed a hospice home. Mom looked over and said, "I don't want to live there."

And she didn't. Not even at the very end.

We arrived at the old farmhouse around 8:00. Tom unloaded the hospital bed and set it up, while we unloaded my mother. Paula got her undressed, gave her a snack, and put her to bed.

The only thing for the three of us to eat was old tortilla chips and grated cheese.

Stale nachos never tasted so good.

UNLOADING

Sitting on the porch that first morning with our coffee, watching the sun come up seemed like a dream. A line of pines spread across the horizon while an open pasture lay before us. Bluebirds landed on a wire, and wrens flitted through the white pine situated in the front yard. I didn't hear cars or horns or chatter. All I heard was God's noise.

After all of the planning and anticipating, we had finally arrived. Now what?

"Let's unload the truck, Pauline." Easier said than done. When we left Florida, we had four strapping men. Now it was just the two of us.

"How? We have some stuff to stay at the farmhouse, but most of it goes into storage until our house is built."

The porch screen door slammed behind Tom as he exited.

I checked in on Mom and Paula. They sat in the cozy room that overlooked the front porch, beginning their breakfast routine.

"How did you sleep?"

"Fine," Mom answered.

I looked at Paula. Her "bedroom" lay underneath the stairs to the attic. The dimensions were about 5' by 10'. We dubbed it

"Harry Potter's room." She just smiled.

"We'll make it better this afternoon."

Tom had four boxes off of the truck by the time I got there. "Help me with the kitchen stuff, okay?" Working all morning, we succeeded in unloading the boxes for the farmhouse. Next, we had to visit the two storage units we'd rented in Dobson.

"How are we gonna get the furniture off the truck?" By the time the words were out of my mouth, Tom had a small table unloaded. And so we worked. And worked. And worked.

"Don't you ever take a break?"

"Why, do you need one?" He grinned.

The last piece of furniture to unload was the center console of our three-piece entertainment center. I'm guessing it weighed 400 pounds. Tom positioned it by the ramp with several straps attached. "Ready? When I say okay, start to gently push it down the ramp onto the dolly."

My hands began to sweat as I pushed. We'd already taken several furniture-moving risks as far as I was concerned. If it were up to me, we'd have hired help. In fact, we discussed that topic at great length at various levels of volume.

I pushed gently and the console slid dangerously to the right before I could stop it. "Watch out!" Tom turned and steadied it to the ground. I almost passed out.

"Why didn't we hire someone?" I shouted in between sobs. "You could have been killed!"

And that chronicled the first of several arguments we would have over how to accomplish even the simplest tasks.

(I was always right, of course.)

THE FARMHOUSE

The house Tom's grandfather built stood in the middle of

three cleared acres, facing a field. White siding added by Tom's mom covered the outside, but underneath the foundation of the house boasted 100-year-old pine and oak. The foundation had crumbled somewhat, so the floor was uneven. Entering through the front porch, you'd see a small hallway to one side and the stairs to the attic on the other. We'd blocked the hallway that led to the bathroom in order to close in "Harry's Room."

On the left, Mom enjoyed the biggest room. Tom had already covered the floor with laminate on his trip earlier in April. The room contained an old fireplace that didn't work, a mantle that did, and a door Tom installed to the bathroom.

The bathroom could have held a bed. This part of the house was added after Tom's mom grew up. Back then, they used the outhouse. The floor had air pockets and tired vinyl, but it worked. A shower, bathtub, and toilet took up about a third of the space so there was a lot of room for Mom to navigate her walker. We were grateful for that.

To the right of Mom's room was the parlor. A sunny room with broad windows and a door leading to the porch, we opted to make that our bedroom. Both of these rooms boasted old time fireplaces that were no longer usable. That was a disappointment.

If you turned right from the front door, you would enter the living area. Paneled and dark, we used it mostly for reading and nighttime gatherings. Tom's mother had used it as a bedroom since it held the only workable air conditioner.

The kitchen ran across the back of the house. Covered with vinyl on both the floor and counters, and the counter fit tightly against a built-in cabinet to the right. A window sat above the counter. The refrigerator lay to the left in a small alcove with a very low ceiling. A shelf held utensils and small appliances. A giant yellow stove from the 1970s sat opposite the counter along with a microwave. There was plenty of room and easy to work in.

A door from the kitchen led to the back porch. It overlooked the woods along the back section of the property and held a beautiful view of the sunset.

It was to be our home for the next five months while our house was constructed.

GETTING SETTLED

After the backbreaking moving-in process, we settled down into kind of a routine. Tom and I would go for a walk to explore various parts of the property. We'd feed carrots to our neighbor's horses and donkey, admire some cows, and marvel at God's creation.

Almost every day, we'd take a trip into town to get supplies and begin some sort of project. Unless, of course, it was raining. Which it was—almost every day.

It couldn't squelch our enthusiasm.

"Time for YouTube University!" Tom stared at a computer screen taking notes and chatting about farm equipment. I continued to nest and oversee Mom's care. We picked out a local doctor, having files sent from Florida and medications updated. We interviewed caregivers and picked a couple of local ladies.

Tom improved "Harry's Room" with a lamp, blow-up mattress, and side table. We began studying seed catalogs.

"We should grow squash, don't you think?"

"Sure," I agreed. "Are they a plant or a bush or a tree?"

"Dunno," Tom admitted. "Let's grow a lot of tomatoes!"

"I know what those look like." And so it went. We dreamed, unpacked, and enjoyed terrific meals on the back porch each evening as the sun set.

Mom adjusted but seemed more and more agitated. One night, I awoke to hear Paula talking loudly to my mom. I guess Mom followed Paula around in the middle of the night with her walker accusing her of all sorts of stuff.

"I don't trust her!" Mom said quite loudly in her authoritative voice. "She's doing bad things!"

I knew the trip would be hard on Mom, but I never guessed she'd turn on Paula.

Time for Paula to go home. We'd hired another caregiver to fill in for Paula and get a caregiving team established. Plus, one of Mom's younger friends would come for a while.

I drove Paula to the airport. "Sorry, Paula. You have been a gift from the Lord."

She smiled. "I know your mom's not thinking right. You have so many options here. I'm so happy for you." We hugged goodbye as I dropped her at the departure gate.

The other caregiver, Jan, got off the plane from Florida, while Paula loaded on.

"You ready, Jan?"

MEETING THE NEIGHBORS

I'd been to Lowe's Home Improvement two times already. Tom's projects were taking a lot of my time and a lot of gas. Situated on the corner of Highway 601 and US 52, it was not only a twisty-turny drive, but it was about nine hilly miles.

I picked up the last set of screws Tom requested and entered the checkout line. Head down, searching for my debit card, I realized someone had spoken to me.

"How are yeehw?"

I looked up to find the cashier staring at me, smiling broadly. "I'm sorry?"

"How are yeehw?" she said politely.

"Um, fine. Yeah, I guess I'm fine. How are you?" I shot back.

"I'm good. Nice weather, ain't it? Did ya find everything

that ya needed?"

That's when it occurred to me. This lady actually did care if I was fine and if I was pleased with her store. "Yes. Yes, I did." I smiled back as I picked up my package and collected my receipt.

"You have a blest day!" she called to me as I left the store.

People were definitely friendlier here than in Florida. And they knew each other. It didn't matter if you were among five people waiting in line, if the cashier knew you or your family, the line stopped until the conversation ceased. And no one seemed to mind.

I guess people weren't in as much of a hurry as in Florida. Heavy traffic in town consisted of the ten cars lined up each Wednesday night at the pizza drive-thru. Or perhaps at five p.m. you might have anywhere from five to ten cars at the main stoplight. Life moved at a slower pace.

People even spoke more slowly. And with a heavy Southern accent. This small-town life was definitely different.

NIGHT ROAMING

"Mom, what do you need?" I asked for the third time that night.

"I've got to find that baby!" Mom said with a worried look.

"Mom, there's no baby. Could you please go back to bed? We all need some sleep."

With her face all scrunched up, Mom looked at me like I was crazy. "I'll tell you what. I'll find the baby and take care of it."

My answer satisfied her, at least for a few hours. Jan and I were both worn out. And Jan had medical problems of her own.

"Are you ready to go home?" I asked her the next morning.

"I think I had better. I love your mom, but I think it's too hard on me physically to stay. I'm sorry."

I understood. Mom hadn't slept for several nights. We reserved Jan's flight, and I took her to the airport and said good-bye. We'd have to depend on our local caregivers to care for Mom during the day, and I'd be on duty each night. Still, I wondered what was wrong. Mom was hallucinating and appeared to be agitated.

One night as Tom and I slept in the room off of the porch, Sam began barking furiously. Tom got up. "Sam, there is nothing out there! Look!" he said, opening the shade to the front porch. "See, there's…Pauline! Your mom is standing on the front porch!"

Sure enough, there was Mom, with her silky grandma cap on top of her white hair, hands on our window, staring in at us. It looked like a scene from *Psycho*.

"What are you doing, Mom?" I said almost angrily, not because I was angry, but because I was scared. Scared that we woke up to a sinister face staring at us in our window, but even more scared that my mother had wandered out on the porch and could have hurt herself.

"I'm looking for that baby!" she replied.

Something had to be done.

The next day, I figured out what was bothering her. She had four herniated discs in her back. For several years, the doctor had prescribed a narcotic patch for pain. In all of the excitement and confusion of moving and settling in, I'd forgotten to change it. Mom was actually going through withdrawals.

I felt terrible. So did Mom. Trying to keep up with all of the changes and supervising Mom's care would be challenging.

One of many challenges I would face in the next few years.

FLEAS, AND TICKS, AND RAIN, OH MY

We couldn't do much outside since it had rained almost the whole month of May and June. It brought out the bugs. Lots of them. In the farmhouse, but especially on our dog, Sam.

"Tom, I want to have a Bible study here to be in God's Word and also get to know some of the ladies better. Plus, it's raining all the time, and I really can't do much else."

"Are you sure you want to have it here?" Tom asked, looking around.

After a long discussion, we decided to try.

I'd made a few friends at church, but everyone was busy. Around my new area, most had extended family. There were ballgames to attend, birthday parties for cousins, and grandmas to visit. Still, Tom and I invited people over several times and had a few takers. I passed out a flyer announcing the study and waited.

The night arrived. "I put signs on the tree outside and moved all of our cars," Tom said.

I had no idea how many to expect. I'd led countless studies before and always enjoyed them. Four wonderful ladies showed up. Although there were just a few of us, we had a marvelous time. Over the next few weeks, I generally had three, but sometimes just two.

About the third week, my neighbor who attended the study said, "I just found a tick on me."

Seriously embarrassed, I helped her remove it.

Then she found another. Time to get serious about bug killing.

"Doctor, the farmhouse is damp, and has indoor-outdoor carpet. I've tried everything to get rid of fleas and ticks, but nothing is working. I'm really at a loss."

"Let me take a look at him," he said as he led Sam into a different room. A few minutes later he returned.

"I've given Sam a peel, and tomorrow, I want you to give him a peel." Then he exited.

How on earth am I going to give a poodle a peel? Sam weighs close to sixty pounds! How would I even do that?

He returned with a small package. It contained a white pill.

"A pill! You want me to give Sam a pill!" I burst out laughing. I laughed all the way to my car. The staff just gawked at me.

DOING THE DISHES

"Hand me the towel, Pauline," Mom said while perched on her sturdy walker.

We'd just finished another tasty dinner on the back porch as the sun tucked in for the night. I cleared, the caregiver washed, and Mom dried. Sometimes we chatted or sang, or sometimes we were silent.

"What shall we have for dinner tomorrow, Mom?"

"Oh, I don't care. Whatever you cook is fine. Maybe I can help you fix dinner. I don't do much around here, and I hate that you have to work so hard."

"You're helping now! Besides, you worked for eighty some years. It's time to take care of you."

"I suppose. Hand me another pan. This one is finished."

After Mom dried, we usually dried the dish again since Mom's hands didn't work correctly. Drying gave her a sense of purpose.

Everyone needs that.

I miss those days of doing dishes together. My new house has a great dishwasher—and that's saying something since usually I hate my appliances. No, I don't miss not having a dishwasher, but doing the dishes together forced me to take time with Mom, doing something automatically. A chore that seemed to lessen when done with others.

Sometimes during those dishwashing evenings, we'd have a serious conversation. Serious conversations work better when you're busy doing something and don't have to look at each other.

Those serious conversations were going to come up more and more over the next few years. I wish we could have been doing the dishes.

GROWING IN CHRIST

Growing up as an OB (Officer's Brat) in the Salvation Army, we moved quite a bit. In fact, to this day, I've lived in seven states and eleven cities. The change was kind of fun and usually a little scary. At one time, when my children were little, my two best friends moved away from me. Devastating would be the word—not only for me—but my children as well. I lost my best friends and they lost theirs. I remember sitting in a neighbor's tree with my daughter looking forlornly at our abandoned friends' house who just pulled out to move to some faraway place known as Cincinnati.

A few months later, out of necessity, I became friends with my two "besties" today. I'm grateful.

Each day when I apply my needed makeup and put on grown-up clothes to go to work, I realize how I've changed over the years. Gravity, sun exposure, and general body breakdown has taken its toll.

Change is part of this world.

One of the attributes of the Lord I appreciate so much is His immutability. In other words, He does not change. In this constantly changing world, that is comforting.

Hebrews 13:8 says, "Jesus Christ *is* the same yesterday, today, and forever" (NKJV).

In my human mind, I cannot imagine forever. I can't fathom a thousand years ago. Sometimes, I can't remember yesterday. But the Bible tells us that the God of the universe not only has never changed, but He will never change.

He is still all-loving, just, holy, all-powerful, all-knowing, righteous, compassionate, slow to anger, and merciful, as He was before time began and will be for eternity. That thought should keep you busy for a few thousand years.

In a world that continues to change, you can count on the One who never changes.

As I write these words, I am thinking about you, my friend. Probably you are facing changes just like I have. Some of them are for good—like a new baby or grandchild. Or a trip to see a loved one you haven't seen for a long time.

Others might be hard, like missing a loved one that has gone to heaven. You might have a wayward child or even a wayward spouse. Or you might be facing an illness.

Count on this—the Lord never changes. If you are His child, He chose you before the foundation of the world. He loves you with an everlasting love. He died to make a way for you to spend eternity with Him.

Amazing love.

Chapter 4

GIFTS

"Every good thing given and every perfect gift is from above, coming down from the Father of lights, with whom there is no variation or shifting shadow." James 1:17

GOING PLACES

*E*verything we did became an adventure.

"You want to go to the dump, Pauline? Then we can head to town and visit Tractor Supply and Lowe's."

"Could we make a stop at Walmart, too?" Tractor Supply, Lowe's, and Walmart were my new mall. Delighted, we loaded our trash into the pickup. In Florida, we placed our messy garbage by the curb two times a week to be miraculously removed by garbage elves. Not on the farm.

"Remember, you can't just put stuff in without weighing it down. It will blow out," Tom said. I readjusted the stuff and got into the front seat. The dump was a "fer piece" down the road. Up Johnson to Siloam, Park, and Sheep Farm Road we traveled, enjoying the view of green pastures, cows, and, of course, sheep.

After several sharp turns, we arrived at the dump and deposited our trash. The attendant studied us as we drove up, said a quick, "Howdy," and inspected our trash to see if we were concealing any unwanted contraband of cardboard or glass.

"See you next week!" we shouted cheerily to the attendant as we drove into town.

"Who knew we'd be driving to the dump..." Tom paused. "And liking it!"

After that, we went to my new mall in our farm boots and sweatshirts. We fit right in. We perused the feed aisle at Tractor Supply, checked out supplies at Lowe's, and purchased plastic containers from Walmart.

That night we were to attend a small-livestock auction. We had no idea what that was but figured we couldn't pass it up. We arrived at the venue and waited in line. Observing the others around me, I could tell they knew what to expect. There was even a concession stand. Most people I saw carried Mountain Dew, a candy bar, and even pork skins. The attendant handed out numbers, and we were ushered through a door into a wide, open barn-like area.

There were several stalls containing goats, chickens, and sheep. All of the stalls had numbers with names. Exiting the barn, we found a place in the stockyard balcony surrounded by others. A family of four sat near us. Several men claimed the back row, sitting on the back of the chairs, boots on the seat.

"I've got five perfectly good laying hens here. Who'll start off the bid?" Then the auctioneer began his chant, which I couldn't understand but everyone else seemed to. To my horror, he plucked one of the chickens out of the box by her feet! No one else seemed astounded by his actions. I guess the crowd wanted a closer look to see if they wanted to bid on the "ladies."

One of the men behind me raised his hand ever so slightly as the first bidder. Soon the auctioneer hit his gavel and pronounced the chickens "Sold" to a couple in the first row. Some teenage helpers carted the hens away while marking the amount and number on a tag and attaching it to the cage.

Next, a metal gadget appeared. I traveled back to the men planted on the back seats. Tom's mouth dropped in shock, but I was gone before he could stop me.

"Excuse me, what are those that the auctioneer is selling?"

Four young men stared hard at me. They wore dusty denim and looked as if they'd all done an honest day's work before they'd arrived at the auction.

"Them are feeders, ma'am."

"Feeders for what?" I asked.

"Chickens." One of the men stood.

"Thank you. We're new in town and this is so exciting for us!"

"Yes ma'am," he answered with a quizzical look.

We didn't stick around for the goats and sheep. As we drove home, we talked about how we never knew about small-livestock auctions, and feeders, and a whole lot of other things.

And we couldn't wait to learn!

SORTING OUT SEEDS

"I want to grow some green beans," Tom stated simply. Trouble was, green beans weren't as simple as they seemed.

"There are a plethora of them," I said nonchalantly.

"Um, that's a big word. So, what are my choices?"

Fifteen seed catalogs surrounded us on the farmhouse table. "That depends on whether you want pole beans, bush beans, filet beans, flat pod beans, soybeans, fava beans, or dry beans," I finished my sentence and drew a deep breath.

"I just want regular green beans," Tom whined.

"No such thing. Just pick a category."

"Okay, how about bush beans. What have you got for me?"

"Well, Johnny's Seeds has Provider, E-Z Pick, Orient, Cosmos, Jade, Amethyst, Royal Burgundy, Carson, and Rocdor. Really, who named that last one?"

Tom looked thoughtful, "Are they all green?"

"Most. There's a mixture called Triology made up of green, yellow, and purple."

"How about we try them?" Tom's eyes lit up.

"They're organic, but it says one will mature before the other. Kind of like girls and boys." I grinned.

"How about another one? Looks like Cosmos is a favorite, but they're not organic. Jade is organic. Wait, it has some letters by it." I squinted, "BMV. IR: BBS, CRM, R."

"What the heck does that mean?"

I brought the catalog closer to my eyes. "Looks like it tells what the plants are resistant to, like rust or mildew or blight."

"What's that mean?"

"Dunno."

And so it continued through several catalogs and many days and even a few disagreements. Finally, we pushed the button and submitted our order. We'd spent over $400.

"I've been looking at seed spreaders," Tom mentioned.

I quoted from an old Disney film *The Lion King*, "Don't start that again!"

CHECKING THE MAIL

Each day we checked our mailbox with great anticipation. I felt like leaving milk and cookies for the mailperson. "Hey, why do you get to open mailbox? You opened it yesterday!"

"Yeah, but I got here first," Tom said as he retrieved the mail before I had a chance. "We got an envelope from Johnny's and a box from Baker's."

"The tomatoes must have come!"

Then we'd skip back to the farmhouse, spread out the seeds, handling them like rare gems.

"Here are the Cherokee Purple, the Mr. Stripey, and Valencia."

"I've got the Roma and Brandywine. Look how pretty they are!" I showed Tom the packet. Reverently, I opened the packet to expose twenty-five baby soon-to-be tomato plants. "Aren't they beautiful?"

From beans to broccoli, from leeks to lettuce, and spinach to squash we categorized, filed, and made seed spreadsheets until our eyes crossed. Time to plan.

We'd purchased giant sized super sticky notes for our fantasy football draft in Florida. No kidding, they are about 2' by 3'. We stuck them to the dining room wall.

"Pauline, this year I think we should do the rows from north to south. We can fit several in the section right in front of the farmhouse. Please draw ten rows of one hundred feet each."

I used a ruler and dutifully drew the rows on the sticky.

"I say we put the tomatoes in the third and fourth rows, and the peppers in row two."

"Why?"

"Because tomatoes and peppers are both night shade plants and they like being near each other. We just can't replant there next year."

"Really. Plants like to be next to each other. I don't believe it," I said.

"Really. It's called companion planting. Some plants like other plants. And some plants don't like other plants."

"Sounds like a plant clique to me. Seriously, Tom, you have really learned a lot. Do you think we can make a living at this?"

"I hope so."

"Let's put cantaloupe and watermelon on row one. I read that the leaves are prickly and deer and other animals don't like to walk on them."

And on and on it went until we had the entire wall covered with giant yellow stickies with our hopes and dreams drawn with a #2 pencil across pretend rows.

SOIL BLOCKS AND COMPOST TEA

"Why are we collecting dead leaves again?"

Tom sighed. "We're collecting leaves to make compost tea. There are a lot of dead leaves in the woods on the property. Using organic matter on plants and in the soil is the best thing we can do to grow good stuff."

"Is this the last wheelbarrowful?" I could hear myself almost whine. We'd already collected four. Tom could work for hours without taking a break or anything—just working.

He headed toward the house. "Yep. This one should do it."

A large garbage can sat on the back lawn. Tom used pantyhose for "teabags." He shoveled dead leaves into the pantyhose, set it in the can, and added water.

"Now what?"

"We let it steep for several days. You want a cup?"

"I'll pass, thanks."

After we made tea, we settled on the back porch to make soil blocks. Soil blocks are dirt mixed with organic matter formed into cubes of various sizes with the use of a simple hand-held machine. The idea is to plant seeds into the blocks and then transfer them to the field when they are mature.

We had several sizes of metal blocks ranging from one to three inches. A large mixing bowl sat between us on the back-porch table. "I don't think I've got the mixture right. The blocks seem to be falling apart," Tom stated. He added more water and something else white.

"What's that?"

"It's perlite. It's an ingredient used in plant growth," he said.

"Do you even sleep? Where do you get all this information?"

"You know those books I bought at the conference? I read them. Plus, I bought all of *Mother Earth News* for the computer."

Shocking! Tom buying more stuff. I noticed our bank account depleting, but hey, everyone needed soil blocks and perlite, right? Besides, we were farmers, and farmers need a lot of stuff. At least I thought they did.

TOM'S BABIES

We began to plant the seeds in the soil blocks to transfer them into the field once they were plant teenagers. Beginning with tomatoes, we chose five different varieties. Tom carefully retrieved the seed with a toothpick, placing it into the block at just the right depth. After tomatoes, we seeded beets, kale, and peppers.

To our delight, all began to sprout except the tomatoes. "I think they're not warm enough," Tom said thoughtfully. I pictured tiny tomato blankets with bunnies on them covering each plant. Turns out, I was wrong.

That night, I went to turn on the lamp. Tomato seeds sat on top of it, warming their little tomato hearts. "Nice," I said.

A few days later Tom said, "Come see!"

On top of the lamp near "Harry's Room," a tiny green stem poked out of the dirt.

"Amazing."

MEETING A FARMER AND HIS COW

A few days later, we visited a local farmer. "We're supposed to meet him at the park and he'll drive us in. Says it's too rough for our truck," I said, following the signs to the park. "Look, there he is!"

"Hey y'all," Josh said with his usual Southern drawl. He's a sturdy man of twenty-five with about fifty years of farming experience. "Hop in!"

"You could spit into Virginia from here," he explained. Although tempted, I declined. We traveled windy roads with a majestic view of low mountains. White knuckled, I hung on. "This land has been in my family for centuries. We have a deed from the king of England."

I couldn't imagine living in one place for generations, but in Surry County that seemed to be the norm.

First, he showed us his bottom land. This land is usually near water. It was covered with a grayish-brown hue much different from our clay soil. Several rows of black plastic hosted healthy plants.

"We'll be harvesting soon. I think there'll be several thousand pounds of squash." He uttered those words as if stating it might rain. I couldn't imagine that much squash. Ever.

"Let's go down and look at the pump." Taking a look at his irrigation system was the reason for our visit.

We hiked through thick brush down a steep embankment to the river. Quiet and cool, I imagined Tom and Huck Finn hanging out there. A large highway passed overhead, and I wondered how many dreamy places I'd missed in my life as I talked on my cell phone, crossing over bridges just like the one above us. The beautiful places no one notices.

Two of his other fields were dotted with contented cows. I'd never been up close to a cow before. I felt small. He let us pet them. Soft and furry, that's how it felt.

Josh fed one older cow Nabs crackers. "We might process some of the herd, but she's our pet," he said. "We're gonna bury her."

We said goodbye with the promise of a dinner out for Josh and his wife. Quietly we rode home over bumpy roads and windy hills as the sun set. We looked forward to our dinner on the porch.

After dinner, we lined up for kitchen duty when Mom's caregiver picked something off of my neck. "It's a tick," she said with a disgusted look on her face.

Tom came out of the bathroom, "I found two ticks on me." I guess that's part of living in the country.

Then we played solitaire, watched fireflies, and exhausted, fell into bed tick free.

A perfect day—minus the ticks.

HEN SITTING AND ROOSTER KICKING

"Sure, we'll feed them while you're away," I told the young couple. They lived in an old mobile home on the property by the farmhouse. "Don't worry about a thing! How much trouble could a couple of chickens and a rooster be?" They headed for the coast in their loaded-down minivan.

Each morning, I'd visit the "ladies" in their pen. Five hens split a six by six area. Outside their pen roamed the forlorn rooster. He bunked down in the dilapidated barn next door. "Hello, ladies, it's time for breakfast! Yes, that means you, too, Sir," I said to the lone rooster.

All seemed content until Friday of that week. "Hello, Sir, how are you this morning?" The rooster must have mistaken my greeting for a threat. He charged directly at me, jumped and kicked me with whatever you call rooster feet. I called for Sam who idled about twenty feet away. He stared apprehensively while keeping his distance.

"Tom! Help! The rooster is attacking me!" Tom worked in the distance, not seeming to notice my call for help.

The rooster persisted, tearing my long shorts just above the knee and drawing blood. Desperate, I took off my $5 Dollar General shoe and smacked him upside his chicken brain. He retaliated with more kicks. I backed up and swung three or four times. Undeterred, the rooster kicked again—kicking the shoe out of my hand.

Kung-fu Rooster.

Finally, he backed off and I stopped sweating.

Smiling, Tom moseyed up. "How'd you make out with the rooster?"

"You saw it and didn't help? I called you when he attacked me!"

"I noticed after the altercation was complete." He grinned. "You've got to toughen up."

At that point, I wished I still had my shoe to throw at him. But then I laughed. "Hey, I'm bleeding. You happy?"

We laughed again. Who knew a small farm could be such a treacherous place?

"Carry a stick next time," he advised.

"Or heavier shoes."

Tom put the rooster away that night. After that, Rooster Sir fasted for much of the week. He needed to toughen up.

GROWING IN CHRIST

There is something about being outside in God's creation that makes you just want to worship—at least it does me. Tom and I marveled at God's natural gifts every single day. God's handiwork trumps man's every time.

Each day as we round the corner to Mount Airy, the Blue Ridge Mountains come into view. An unrehearsed gasp erupts from my mouth. As we view rolling hills filled with livestock, I am filled with amazement and peace as calves nurse peacefully or lambs frolic in the fields. I ask the Lord to never let me lose my wonder at His handiwork.

Shepherd David spent all his early years out among the sheep, gazing at the stars. Some of my favorite psalms are from that time in his life. Here are a few verses that express his praise to the Lord for His creation and provision:

"Sing to the LORD with thanksgiving; sing praises to our God on the lyre, Who covers the heavens with clouds, Who provides rain for the earth, Who makes grass to grow on the mountains. He gives to the beast its food, And to the young ravens which cry" (Ps. 147:7–9).

C.S. Lewis suggests looking down to appreciate the magnificence of the Lord. The delicacies of a flower, the intricacies of a ladybug, the texture of a blade of grass. All paint a picture of the Great Creator.

You may live in a big city and have trouble finding a sprig of grass. Or maybe you live by the beach. Take time to notice God's creation. Look down at the intricacies of a ladybug. Admire a stately tree. Take time for a walk on the beach or to watch a colorful sunset.

I can't think of a better way to destress in a stressful world. Admiring God's creation also tends to instill gratefulness instead of grumpiness.

It may even stir praise in you for the One who deserves it.

Chapter 5

FAITH

*"Never be afraid to trust an unknown future
to a known God." ~ Corrie ten Boom*

THE GREEN MACHINE

One of the implements we purchased for our tractor we dubbed the Green Machine. This baby builds raised beds, lays irrigation tape, covers the beds in white plastic, and covers the edges of the plastic in dirt. The day came for us to try it out.

My friend Miriam and her mother had arrived to help for a week. We lingered along the edge of the field as Tom took his first swipe with the Green Machine. It stuck in the dirt. Tom climbed out, readjusted a few bolts and knobs and climbed back up.

Miriam pulled out her phone. "There he goes!" she shouted.

The hot white sun beat down on chunky red clay. Tom started the tractor, checked the machine, climbed up, and gave us the thumbs-up sign.

The tractor lurched forward and straightened. The machine pulled steadily behind, laying a bumpy white slather of plastic piled high above the good earth.

"Yahoo!" we shouted, jumping up and down. "It works! It really works!" We whooped and hollered and high-fived, grins spread wide across our faces.

"Start planting!" Tom yelled with cupped hands from the tractor, face glowing.

Miriam and I ran into the house and looked at the seed map written on the yellow stickies stuck to the farmhouse wall. "What do we plant first?" she asked.

"Let's start with squash!" We retrieved five different kinds of the vegetable and stared at them. "Now what?"

"Let's YouTube it," suggested my friend. Back to the computer screen and out to the field, we toted our seeds, gleefully embracing our plant calling.

"You start on that side and I'll begin on this side of the row."

As we poked the seed into the rocky, dry clay, my smile gradually faded. I looked up at my close friend who knew me and loved me no matter what and said, "What have we done?" We'd pulled up stakes from friends and family in one of the most beautiful places in America; we'd sold all and invested all in our new farm venture.

Now, dear reader and new friend, I know you are thinking people, who recycle your trash in neat bins and have a 401K account. You may not understand this next statement I am about to say. But here it is:

Until that very day, there was not one doubt in my mind that we would succeed as farmers. Not only did I believe we would succeed, but I believed we would make loads of money.

Let's switch back to you neat trash sorters. Don't get me wrong—I love you. But you probably wouldn't have had my thoughts because you would have had a five-year business plan. I had a faith plan—*my* faith plan. Let me explain.

Since the Lord gave us the land, and the desire of our heart was to share with others both monetarily and through hospitality, I assumed God would bless us financially. And I believed He would do this miraculously. Big time. Without much effort on our part.

I'd like you to hold that thought as I continue with our adventure. My irrational thinking is important because I assumed my plan was God's plan instead of trusting Him with a perfect plan.

LIVING THE DREAM

Despite my ineptness, and in spite of my chutzpa, even when it rained for days and days with no sun, tiny shoots stretched up through rocky soil. In fact, beautiful yellow flowers unfolded before our eyes, promising tasty squash. My enthusiasm for farming was renewed.

I also began conversing with the plants. "Okay, little beet, time to grow up. Can't let a strong wind knock you down. It's a tough world out here. Put your roots down deep." I worked in silence with just the wind seeping through poplars.

Our new life continued and soon our old life on a quarter acre seemed a distant dream. Each day began with coffee, of course. I did miss sitting in comfy chairs at Starbucks, but I wouldn't trade my new life for my old.

Tom and I were living a dream.

Our daughter and her husband came for a visit in July and slept on a blow-up mattress under the stairs in "Harry's Room."

"Don't you love it here?" we asked expectantly, smiles wide, resting on the edge of our chairs.

Sitting on the old farmhouse porch, gazing out onto the field with sumo wrestler-sized bees hovering at eye level they looked at each other. "We're happy for you!" They managed to say.

"Can you see the squash blossoms in the field? Let's go see them!" I popped up.

"That's okay, Mom, remember we saw them yesterday," Sarah said politely.

We understood they are not and never will be country people, so we took them to a beautiful winery in Virginia with a breathtaking view and bought them lunch. They were content, and we were happy since our bank account still held money from our house and boat sale.

We showed them pictures of our house layout, the cleared land, and the brick foundation that stood at the site. "They're going to bring the house in within a few weeks! We've opted for hickory floors and a few upgrades, and get this—we are going to have a 10' by 60' front porch so we can have loads of company!"

We couldn't stop smiling as they drove off the next day. In fact, we couldn't stop smiling every day. And soon, we'd have our first harvest. We couldn't wait!

OUR FIRST SALE

Although we had baby plants, our work had just begun. We weeded, seeded, and de-bugged each day for several hours. My nails were constantly dirty and my hair unkempt.

The bugs were especially challenging. "Don't kill that bug, it's an assassin bug and it helps plants!"

"Are you trying to tell me there are good bugs and bad bugs, and that a good bug is called an assassin bug?" I asked incredulously.

"Yes, Pauline."

"So, I guess the flea beetles aren't good since we are trying to drown them in beer?"

"That is correct," Tom replied in all seriousness. Along the outside of our field where collards grew, we had filled tiny lids with beer since Tom read it attracted flea beetles, and they'd drown after they flew into one. In spite of our efforts, the flea beetles continued to munch on our collards, but we thought we heard some of them singing happy choruses, buggy arms interlaced, swaying back and forth on our collard leaves.

Because of the bugs, we didn't have much to take to the local co-op, but we had some vegetables, and they were beautiful.

Solemnly, we cut our first yellow squash and zucchini, thanking God for His goodness and our harvest.

"Have you got everything packed up, Pauline?"

"Yep. Two kinds of squash, some arugula, heirloom zucchini, and a handful of okra." I looked lovingly at our produce. I couldn't believe we had grown actual food. Not only that, we had sampled some for dinner on the back porch the previous evening, and it was heavenly!

Loading into the truck we drove the twelve miles to the local co-op, toting our goods. The young farmer met us there. "That is some mighty pretty squash!" he said.

We glowed with delight. Then he wrote us our first check as farmers—a whopping $5.87.

We were still glowing as we got back into the truck, but it had lost a little of its luster. "Let's see, about an $80K investment, numerous man hours, and $10 worth of gas," Tom said.

We laughed all the way home.

CHECKING ON THE CHICKS

The phone jolted us awake at about 6:05 a.m. My eyes scrunched at the bedroom light as Tom answered. "Yes, this is the Hylton residence. Yes, that's right. We'll be right there." Turning to me, like an expectant father he announced, "They're here!"

Jumping out of bed, I gathered my shorts and a T-shirt from the previous day and dressed quickly. We'd planned everything.

I'd go into town to the post office, and Tom would stay home with Mom and make last minute preparations for the chicks.

Tom continued, "They said to go to the back door of the building and knock hard."

Our eyes held for a moment. "Here I go. See you when I get back!" I gave Tom a quick hug, the back door slamming behind me.

I pulled behind the post office, got out of the car, and knocked hard. A middle-aged woman in blue answered, "Yes?"

"The name is Hylton. I'm picking up a package."

She smiled, "Oh yes, they're over there near the light." She walked over to the table and handed me two pizza boxes filled with seventy-five, day-old chicks.

Knowing the chicks were fragile and had to be kept at about 95 degrees, I covered the boxes with blankets, making sure the air holes were clear, and raced home. "Little chicks, you're going to your new home at Peeled Poplar Farm. You're going to love it there. We have an apartment called a brooder waiting with fresh cedar shavings and a warm light. You'll get to meet your brother, Sam—he's a big poodle, and Tom, he's my husband. We're going take good care of you."

Tom met me at the door. "Hurry, let's get them under the light!" And with that we opened our two pizza boxes filled with three different varieties of tiny chicks. They piled out of their boxes and into our lives. None of our lives would ever be the same.

We checked on them several times during the night and into the next day.

The first thing we experienced was a death. Two of the chicks didn't make it. We understood this often happens, but it still made us sad.

"Good morning to you, good morning to you, good morning, dear chickies, and good afternoon, too!" I'd sing as I checked on the chicks. Their brooder sat covered in blankets, resting on the back porch. In the evening, I'd sing "Good night, ladies, good night, ladies, good night, ladies, it's time to say goodnight."

They would entertain Tom and me for hours with their antics as they grew. One day they fit neatly in pizza boxes, the next day they doubled in size. By the end of the first week, we knew they needed more room, so we opened the chicken door to the other section of the brooder. That lasted a few weeks, too.

"We can't keep them in this brooder much longer," Tom said. "I'm going to need to build something bigger. While I do that, let's move them to the back yard. We can surround the brooder with a fence or something like that."

Using movable fencing, we fashioned a makeshift pen around the brooder on the back lawn. "What about hawks?" I asked.

We decided to use our new farmers market tent, kept low to the ground to cover them, with the fencing attached by wire ties. A chicken bridge was added, stretching from the ground up to the brooder so they could settle in at night. It would do as Tom began to build the coop.

Choosing a Quonset hut design, he purchased wood and metal siding and began to build. Tom's favorite thing in the whole world is to build things. He whistled and hummed and after a few days he finished. I don't know how much money we put into the coop, but I believe it could withstand a nuclear explosion.

Finally, chicken moving day came. The hens or "ladies" were ready to nest. Sam waited expectantly as we gathered the chicks. We made several swoops around the fence trying to catch the girls. Several crafty ones escaped. An hour and a half later most of the chicks arrived at their new digs.

Unfortunately, in all the excitement, Sam stepped on one and broke its back. I cupped the little chick in my hands as I sat on the back-porch steps; she looked up at me and peeped pitifully. Staring into those helpless chicken eyes, I sobbed. "I'm so sorry, little chicken. I'm so sorry!" The caregiver watched from the back porch and brought me a tissue. Wiping my face on my dirty T-shirt, I knew what had to be done, but I couldn't do it.

I looked at Tom. He cradled the chick in his arm and walked to the woods. Those few days and weeks became difficult lessons in the tremendous responsibility of caring for livestock. There are great times of joy but also times when you have to do hard things. Putting that little chicken out of its misery was a really hard thing for Tom.

Once the ladies moved in, the hens grazed cheerily on the green grass. The trouble began when they roosted for the night. Although they lived near the Taj Mahal of chicken coops, they refused to move in.

That was unacceptable. Mostly because everything in the world likes chicken, including me—and probably you. These predators were especially active at night. The chickens needed the added protection of being locked in their coop each evening.

So, before sundown, Tom and I chased hens around the pen until we had them loaded into the coop so they would learn where to bunk at night. The entire process took about forty-five minutes.

"How long have we been doing this?" I asked Tom.

"About five days."

"Do we have dumb chickens?" I hated to even think it.

One evening, we came home late from a farm show. The chickens were piled up in various corners of the pen, outside the coop. Tom picked our sleeping hens up one by one and handed them to me in the coop. Gently, I placed them on the floor or on their perches. The whole process took about five minutes.

We learned something that evening. After chickens go to sleep, you can basically vacuum and they hardly budge.

We learned something else, too. Our chickens weren't the ones who were dumb.

A HOUSE RAISING

Tom and I sat in weathered plastic chairs as a tractor and crane pulled the two pieces of our forever home onto our home site. Taking the day off of farming, we figured it wasn't every day you get to see your house "put together."

The crane lifted one piece of our modular home and placed it securely on our brick foundation. Several men did all kinds of work I didn't understand. That took about an hour, and then we held our breath as the crane lifted the other half and nestled it next to the first. The men attached the two pieces together, did a few cosmetic things and moved on to the roof.

Viewing the house-raising got even more interesting when the crane secured pieces attached to each side of the building and magically pulled up a roof. Tom held his cell phone, preserving our memory. Within a few hours, we faced a house that we would call home.

Clinking our water bottles together in celebration, we entered our front door by way of a ladder—otherwise Tom would have carried me across the threshold. We'd seen the inside before since it sat in our driveway for a week before the construction began. The kitchen contained finished cabinets, a serve-over bar with a marble looking pattern, a pantry, and room for appliances. Windows dotted each wall of the house— many 6' tall and 3' wide. We'd paid extra to have 9' ceilings and our roof sat at a higher angle than most.

For looking at a diagram, taking thirty minutes to pick counters and bathroom flooring, windows, and cabinets, we "done" good. Only the finish work, painting, and at the very end, hickory floors, would be added, and then the Hyltons and Ma Wert would move…again.

This time for good.

Tom and I peered through the windows of the front room, arm in arm. Overlooking a stunning valley complete with cows, we sighed, thanked the Lord for the wonderful opportunity, and went back to work.

ADDING TO OUR FAMILY

Move-in day came in early October. Mom's friend Berta kept her company while Tom and I toted our stuff for the fourth time—thank the Lord. Our porch finished, we rested in our shiny black rockers as the sun slid beneath crisp pines.

"I can't believe we actually live here," I mused, sipping decaf. "I wish our chickens would start laying. I guess we can expect eggs by Christmas. I think we are going to have to invest in those livestock guardian dogs. Someone on the mountain raises them."

"Yeah. Plus, I think there might be rats trying to get in under the house. We need a few mousers."

That conversation would be the catalyst to add more to our farm family. A few days later, I drove almost to the Virginia line to pick up a Great Pyrenees puppy. These dogs are massive white balls of fur whose solitary goal in life is to guard livestock. I watched as the five-month-old puppies ran through the fields, playing with the sheep.

"How much for two?"

I loaded two sisters into my van for the twenty-five-minute trip home. Trouble was, not only had they never been out of the field, they'd never been in a car. Both dogs deposited their dinners on my van floor. After their "present," I decided a trip to the vet would be in order. But the dogs had never been on a floor either. The vet helper and I dragged them since the leash was useless.

After arriving home, Tom asked, "Why do you have two?"

"I didn't want one to be by itself."

Tom shook his head.

I wondered how to hold them until we deposited them with the chickens. "Let's secure them under the porch for now," I suggested. We wrapped chicken wire around the porch while the dogs got used to our farm.

I named the biggest Molly, and Tom named her sister Lacey. All of a sudden, we had dogs with a job. I'd read enough about them to know I couldn't put them in with the chickens right away so we set up the bendable electric fence next to the chicken coop.

The next morning, as soon as we put the girls inside the electric fence, the dogs bounded for the fence, yelped, disappeared into the doghouse Tom fashioned for them, and didn't come out for two days.

After they ventured from their doghouse, I began their training. "Come on, Molly and Lacey, let's go meet the ladies. Your job is to guard them." Molly licked my hand, while Lacey eyed me suspiciously. At first, they were reluctant with the hens, but after a few days entering the hens' section, they began to chase the ladies for fun.

"No!" I said firmly, and then rewarded them when they obeyed. This went on for a few weeks. The dogs began to fit nicely into the Peeled Poplar family. What I hadn't counted on was how hard it would be for me to leave two dogs outside, away from my home. All my life, dogs were part of the family.

"Do you think they're okay?" I asked Tom as we lay in bed, with only stars shining through our windows.

"They're fine, Pauline. They've always lived in a field. They're working dogs."

Still, I worried.

Next on our list were mousers. "Do you know of any kittens that need a home?" I asked my friend Kelly at church one day.

Her face brightened. "I'm glad you asked! My son found two that he is housing in the barn. Their mom is dead. They need a good home."

And with that we brought home two small kittens to our large front porch. They were tiny brothers that we named Reep and Cheep, after C.S. Lewis's courageous Narnian mouse, Reepicheep.

Reep had black lips and a black and white body, while Cheep's coat boasted shiny black fur with a touch of white. Both fit nicely into our family.

Often, in the evening, Mom would sit on our 5' porch swing with us as Reep snuggled in her lap. Cheep took turns with a variety of laps, pushing his head against our hands, purring like a Chevy.

The animals were the beginning of our dream. Although Tom and I didn't have a laid-out business plan, we did have an idea of not only a farm, but also a lifestyle. A lifestyle of working hard and sharing much. A "Whole Farm" with vegetables, fruit, chickens, and eventually cows, pigs, sheep, or goats, and, of course, dogs and cats. We pictured a plentiful harvest with green pastures filled with lively animals.

And then we'd add people—lots of them. We'd encourage a sense of community and I'd have a lot of friends. I began to pray for cabins so anyone who wanted to get away could visit. I knew the Lord would answer an unselfish prayer like that.

And when the people would come, we'd give them eggs and fresh food, and at night we'd all eat together either on the porch or inside, depending on the weather. I told everyone that I knew what the Lord was going to do for us.

I had a lot to learn.

A CELEBRATION

We settled into winter with plans swimming in our heads. The days were short so farm work was at a minimum. Each day we'd hike to the chickens. I'd do the feed, and Tom would fill containers with water. We'd both pet the dogs. I brought them into the hen house with me as I searched for eggs. And each day, we came up empty.

Until just a few days before Christmas.

"Tom! Guess what! I found an egg! It's big and brown and beautiful!" We gawked in amazement at our treasure. After a few days we had enough to share.

Time to celebrate!

"Hey guys! What are you doing for Christmas?" I asked my friends from church.

"We've got plans for Christmas morning, but other than that, we're free."

On Christmas Eve, we shared our table with friends from church. We held hands, thanked the Lord for His gift of Jesus, our friends, and our food.

"What do you want in your omelets?" Tom asked each one.

And with that simple meal, we ate the best omelets in the world, made with fresh eggs from our ladies.

And both our hearts and stomachs were full.

GROWING IN CHRIST

My faith meter was really high then. Fresh eggs, new friends, a new house. Everything was great, and I congratulated myself on my belief that God was in control of our lives. But is that real faith?

Hebrews 11:1 describes faith from God's point of view,

"Now faith is the assurance of *things* hoped for, the conviction of things not seen." The rest of the chapter gives us biblical examples of men and women who exhibited great faith. It's definitely worth the read.

As a follower of Christ, I see two kinds of faith—saving faith and every-day-life faith.

Saving faith is when we hear the gospel of Jesus Christ. That He was and is God, He came to earth as a man, shed His blood on the cross for our sins, and was raised to life proving that His sacrifice paid for our sins. We believe those facts and repent. It is the channel God uses to rescue us. Our only job is to believe. He does the rest.

That is where the daily faith comes in. Trusting God with all aspects of our lives. Believing He cares for us and controls all things. It seems easy to have faith when all is going well. It is more difficult to believe all those things when circumstances don't seem to go our way.

Over the next few years, I would learn more about faith and even my lack of it. I would also see my need for dependence on the Lord. And that's a good thing. A hard thing, too.

How is your faith meter? A little low?

There is a story in Mark 9 about a man who had a son that was demon possessed and ill. The man asked the disciples to heal his son, but they could not. Then he approached Jesus. Here is an excerpt:

"How long has this been happening?" Jesus asked the boy's father.

He replied, "Since he was a little boy. The spirit often throws him into the fire or into water, trying to kill him. Have mercy on us and help us, if you can."

"What do you mean, 'If I can'?" Jesus asked. "Anything is possible if a person believes."

The father instantly cried out, "I do believe, but help me overcome my unbelief!" (verses 21–24 NLT)

The good news is—you can ask Jesus to help you have faith. I do it all the time. I get on my knees and say, Lord, I believe, help my unbelief.

He is a good Father. And He loves to give good gifts to His children. Count on it.

What is one area of your life that could use a faith boost? Why don't you write it down and then ask God to increase your faith in that area? Why not memorize Romans 10:17 or Hebrews 11:1. To have faith, we need to know what His Word teaches and then believe it.

Chapter 6

DOUBT

"But when you ask, you must believe and not doubt, because the one who doubts is like a wave of the sea, blown and tossed by the wind." James 1:6 NIV

LEMONS AND CHICKEN PIE

What do you want to do for your birthday?" I asked Tom as we drove over to take care of the chickens.

"Really, Pauline, I don't care. I know we don't have a lot of extra money to go out."

January was cold and snowy. In fact, we measured 21" in our front yard. Mom kept reminding me that I told her it never snowed here. Not only did we get a mammoth amount of snow for this area, we'd had almost arctic temperatures. By the time Tom's birthday rolled around, it was 17 degrees.

As we drove up to the white fencing, I noticed the ladies all lined up by the fence, waiting for their breakfast. I glanced over at Molly and Lacey whose fence connected with the chicken fence. Something didn't look right.

The dogs sat bolt upright, tails wagging like windshield wipers, with loads of black feathers sticking out of their mouths.

"Wow."

"I'll go feed the chickens," I offered.

While I spread feed and filled water buckets with hot water since theirs was frozen, I heard Tom scolding the puppies. "Bad girls! You're not supposed to eat the chickens, you're supposed to guard them!" Their tails wagged even more brusquely. I guess what happened was a lady hopped over into the dog pen to check things out. She quickly figured out the grass isn't always greener on the other side.

When are we going to get the hang of this livestock life? We'd already invested a gazillion dollars, along with hundreds of manpower hours, and we didn't seem to be able to manage it.

The life of a farmer sure seemed complicated.

We trudged back to the truck. "If we were brave, we'd go get that chicken and eat it. She wasn't dead—I had to kill her. They'd just held her down and played with her. I threw her in the woods."

"Let's do it, Tom! No reason to let the animals have her. We probably have $20 invested in that bird!"

With that, we marched down to the woods, put the hen in a bucket and drove home. Now what? I phoned a friend.

"Kelly, we have a chicken I need to process. How do I do it?"

"Get off as many feathers as you can, dunk it in hot water, get the rest of the feathers off, and then gut it," my farmer's wife friend stated.

The caregiver helped me pull, dunk, pull again, and then gut. Funny, after we finished that process, our chicken looked just like all the other chickens on the grocery aisle. I boiled it, added vegetables and a crust. Voila! Two chicken pies.

When I became a farmer's wife, I had no idea I'd be plucking and cooking a chicken. In fact, I'd never thought much about my food, where it came from, who harvested it, or even if it was treated humanely.

Now I know how much work it takes to cultivate the land,

plant a seed, and harvest a head of lettuce. I understand how the tomatoes on my sandwich are pruned and fed. And now I've a glimpse into the complicated life of owning livestock.

I now have a context when I use the phrases, "you reap what you sow," and "there is a pecking order."

For Tom's birthday dinner, we decided to eat my very first farm-to-table chicken potpie.

In fact, I made up my own saying, "When life hands you lemons, make chicken pie.

After that, I understood another phrase: "She's a tough old bird." That she was. May she rest in peace.

HOOP HOUSES AND RAISED BEDS

"Throw the tennis ball over the top, Pauline."

"Okay. Are you sure this is going to work?" I asked. We wrapped the plastic around the tennis ball and secured it with a rubber band. The plan was to get on both sides of the structure and hoist the plastic, which was connected to the tennis ball, over the top.

"That's what it showed on the video," Tom answered.

Tom had bought metal pipes and a pipe bender and fashioned the ribs of the structure on the back of his truck. He secured the ribs into the ground outside our bedroom window and cut thick plastic to fit.

The tennis ball was attached to a long string so when Tom threw the ball with the plastic over the skeleton of the home-made hoop house, I grabbed the string and secured it to the bottom of the frame. (For you non-farm people, a hoop house is a greenhouse without heat.)

That brought us to the next part. In order to secure the plastic from strong wind, the plastic had to be fastened to the metal.

I tossed a rock wrapped with string to Tom who tightened the string to the base, wound it through the poles and then tossed it back to me. We repeated this process many times. After several hours, the plastic seemed tight and I called it a day.

Not Tom.

He drew patterns for the door and figured the best way to enter the hoop house while at the same time protecting it from the southern winds that travel through the valley and up to our home site. After a few days, the project stood completed.

Instead of basking in his accomplishments, Tom began mapping out raised beds in our yard in front of the hoop house. He studied YouTube, checked out various websites, and began construction.

"How do you like this one, Pauline? I constructed it out of the old logs on the property, cut niches so they fit together. It's kind of like a short, roofless log cabin." Tom beamed.

"It's beautiful, Tom."

His face darkened. "I'm not sure I like the style." And off he went to explore more sites. A few days later he showed me a different one made from planks. "This one is made from boards I got from that old barn."

Since we'd moved to the farm, I hadn't really realized how creative Tom was and how much he enjoyed building his ideas.

"I have one more idea. I'll need your help."

We traipsed out to the woods with a cutter. "We are looking for baby poplar trees. About an inch or two thick." We cut down several and hauled them to our yard.

Tom drove stakes in the ground exactly two feet apart in a big rectangular 4' by 12' pattern. I know this because I waited and helped while he measured, measured again, and then measured a third time before pounding them in. After he finished, he said, "You hold this tree we cut down low to the ground, and I'm going to weave it between the stakes."

Once he began to weave, I understood the pattern. Together, we weaved a beautiful raised bed all from small trees on our property. The result was astounding.

"That's my favorite, Tom. You did a great job!"

He shrugged. "We've got a hoop house and six raised beds. I guess we'd better get busy."

GAIN AND LOSS

"How many broccolis should we start?" I asked Tom while retrieving the folder marked broccoli.

"How many do we have?"

"About 10,000 seeds."

"We like broccoli," Tom said, grinning.

"Not that much."

We ended up filling twenty trays with fifty compartments.

We'd made the decision to go commercial during the farming season. A new cooperative had opened up that sold in bulk to high-end grocery stores. It would give us an avenue to grow a lot of one product and deliver it to one place. Making cold calls had secured the top restaurants in Surry County as my customers, but it was hit-or-miss. I had also begun selling eggs to a local store. But we needed a lot more income to succeed as farmers.

Satisfied with our mega-seeding, we moved on to cabbage. Opting for half red, half green, we planted 500 of each. Next, we filled one or two trays of flowers, kale, collards, and beets. We placed our baby seeds on tables Tom had constructed out of pallets that we picked up for free from the back of Lowe's Home Improvement.

Several times a day, Tom visited the hoop house, checking the temperature, closing or opening the doors, adding water or nutrients. He also purchased a thermometer that reflected the temperature of the hoop house on another thermometer stationed in our bedroom. This was in case the temperature dropped suddenly during the night or rose significantly during the day.

My son's wedding would be held in mid-March, so we'd booked our flights. We entrusted our plants, animals, and mother to my friend Sue and the other caregivers.

"Call us if you have questions. Just make sure and water the plants, Sue. Thanks!"

We said our goodbyes and boarded the plane. Arriving in Clearwater seemed surreal. Pulling out of the airport with our friend put us back in "Big City Mode." The traffic zoomed around us as we pulled out on US 19. We passed the shopping center with my favorite sandwich shop. I noticed a letter burnt out in the grocery store I frequented. We fit right back into the crowded, touristy way-of-life. Because it was our life for over thirty years. It almost seemed like we'd never left.

We attended the wedding held in a garden, celebrated with friends, and boarded the plane for home. After we arrived, our new surroundings seemed unnatural. We felt out-of-place as we pulled into our driveway.

After greeting Mom and checking on the chickens, Tom went out to the hoop house. When he returned, his shoulders slumped. "All the seeds died."

While in Florida, the temperatures on the farm had fluctuated from well below freezing, up into the high fifties. The hoop house registered over 100 degrees.

This had been our first trip away from the farm. We left on a Thursday and returned on a Sunday. It was the first time I wondered how often we would be able to go anywhere or do anything.

And I didn't like it.

ORDERING ONLINE

We replanted some seeds and began our new season. Still, we desired to have asparagus and fruit. Searching the Internet, I found an asparagus expert at a cooperative extension. He encouraged me to buy asparagus crowns that were a year old.

"Most people start with crowns. You plant them and they come up the next year. But you shouldn't harvest any that year. The following year you can harvest some, but not a lot," the man added. I picked his brain for an hour and requested more information.

After weeks of discussion, we decided to place our order. Tom sat in front of our computer screen and scrolled through the commercial plants found on the site. "Let's see, they have blueberries, blackberries, strawberries, all kinds of stuff. They even have rhubarb!"

"I love rhubarb!" My mouth puckered at the thought.

"Why don't we order some of each? Let's start with blackberry bushes. They have fourteen varieties." We perused through the list and read information about each. We decided on two varieties after consulting several of our books, too.

Blueberries had even more choices. That decision took about an hour, so did the strawberry decision. Rhubarb had only a few choices, so we picked only two. Four hours had gone by and we still hadn't ordered asparagus.

Asparagus was one crop no one in the area grew. And we loved it. "Okay," Tom said, "it says there are male and female asparagus."

"Yep. Stay away from the female, buy all male hybrids. (Sounds like a great name for a magazine.) Males are strong and don't give off some kind of stuff at the end of the season that the females do. Trust me on this," I said.

Tom eyed me suspiciously. "Do we want green or purple?"

"Yes."

"How many?"

Before we knew it, we'd ordered 25 blackberry bushes, 25 blueberry bushes, 25 strawberry plants, 25 rhubarb plants, and 1500 asparagus crowns.

Yes, you read that right—1500 asparagus crowns.

It is very easy to click buttons on the computer. We would soon find out that planting them is much more difficult.

THE ASPARAGUS PLANTING

We wondered why the commercial growing company made such a big deal about the actual day the plants would be delivered. On April 24, 2014, we figured that out. All the plants arrived on the same day, all needed to be kept cold and planted ASAP. Tom and I gaped at each other.

Then we emptied our big freezer, turned it down to just above freezing, and stored the asparagus. We spent the next several hours discussing where to plant everything. I'm a quick decision maker, while Tom takes forever. My kids always complain how they fall asleep during his turn at board games because it takes him so long. It was the same with planting.

It was a big decision. You see, asparagus take about three years to get going, but they are perennials that can bloom anywhere from seven to twenty-five years. And it's almost impossible to move them. In fact, all the plants we ordered would continue to bloom year after year. That is, if we could plant as soon as possible and keep them alive after we planted them.

After much debate, we decided to plant the asparagus first. We would plant some in the field behind the tree line in back of our new house and some in the field in front of the old farmhouse.

And they weren't easy to plant. Tom used our green machine and made raised beds without plastic on top. He followed up with the potato plow attachment that dug a big trench in the center of the bed. The trench cut about 9" deep. The idea was to plant the crowns, cover with some dirt and then mulch and add more mulch over time.

The crowns resembled something like a deformed octopus, having a sort of head with what looked like tentacles extending from them that were actually roots. To plant each crown, we had to be on our knees. We spread the roots out in the trench with the head up. Then we covered the entire plant with a few inches of red clay. After that, we scooted over to the next plant.

This wasn't smooth, soft compost-like ground. The red clay held all kinds of rocks and earth clods both in the trenches and also in the rows where we knelt. And knelt. And knelt. Each day we would begin between 9:00 and 10:00 and stopped at dark. Big welts and scratches adorned my knees and legs. My feet began to ache and my temper rose.

"Why did we order all this asparagus, and why do you get to hand them to me while I plant?" I said with a snarky tone of voice, bent over the asparagus row with a filthy T-shirt, torn rooster shorts, and clay-colored hands. "My nails will never be the same! I can't even get the dirt out anymore!"

"You are the one who clicked the button, Pauline, not me!" He noticed my expression and quickly added, "Let's change and you spread the crowns out and I will plant for a while."

After seven grueling days, we finished the asparagus planting. I considered it a success since we remained alive and still married.

The following week consisted of throwing the rest of the plants in the ground. Frankly, by then we didn't care—we were just ready to be finished. Our backs were, too.

The entire process stretched over about two weeks. Each night we hobbled back to the house, ate a quick dinner prepared by the caregiver, and plopped into bed.

"Are we having fun yet?" Tom asked on the last great planting evening after the lights were out.

We fell asleep laughing.

NEW CUSTOMERS AND MARKET SALES

As the season progressed, Tom and I naturally fell into job assignments. Tom took on maintenance and production while my talents seemed to fall into sales and marketing. I would supervise Mom's care in the morning, help Tom for a few hours, and then try to figure out how to make money and prepare for market. Farming was well and good but eventually our money would run out. And it seemed to be running out faster and faster.

We had worked closely with the local cooperative extension, so I signed up for the farmers markets they supported. Tuesday, Thursday, and Saturday. I planned to attend the market while Tom stayed home and worked.

I bungled through the first few markets with a couple of tables, our Peeled Poplar banner, a few vegetables, and some eggs. I wasn't alone. Not many of the farmers had much. Only those with greenhouses produced many varieties and any kind of quantity. I'd attended meetings and met some of the venders that sold not only vegetables, but dog treats and products, jellies, goat soaps, and even leather products.

I was the rookie. Hardly anyone stopped at my booth while the other venders seemed to be on a first name basis with many of the customers. Plus, our products were organic and higher priced than others. I made sure the people knew we sold organic, but many didn't seem to care.

Those first few weeks at market were lonely. When I packed the few products I hadn't sold, I decided to make a few cold calls to local restaurants.

I crept up the stairs of the local high-end restaurant, box of mismatched vegetables in my hand. "Hello, my name is Pauline Hylton, and my husband and I are new organic farmers. I'd like to give you some samples," I said to the head chef and owner. I also handed him a card. He smiled and thanked me as I headed out the door.

That wasn't too hard, I thought. Growing up in the Salvation Army, I was used to door-to-door fund-raising and ringing the bell at the red kettle. After each market, I collected my leftover goods, contacted the local high-end restaurants, gave them a card and left samples.

It paid off. Many chefs welcomed local products. I remember my first sale. "How much do you want for all of them?" the chef asked.

"How much will you pay me?"

Soon, I knew the top head chefs in the county and began to sell to each. The problem was, I never knew what we could grow or keep from the bugs. One chef said, "Let me know what you are growing and I will put it on my menu."

I told Tom.

"The trouble is, we don't know if we can grow stuff and grow enough for him. I don't think we're ready for that, Pauline."

He was right. I made a few bucks and a lot of friends at the restaurants, but not enough money to make a huge difference. I visited a few stores in the area and sold eggs and a few other products to them. I had the right idea, and frankly I was surprised other farmers didn't approach them. We just didn't have the know-how to really support those sales on a regular basis.

THE SALSA LADY

One idea that swam around in our brains was my salsa.

Everyone loved it and said we should market it. As a result, I'd attended a three-day class in Asheville on food safety. That class supposedly made it okay for me to produce salsa. But could I make it in my home? One agency said yes, one said no. The main rule was no animals in our home. That meant Sam could no longer live in our house. On Easter Sunday night, we kicked our faithful dog, Sam, out onto our front porch.

I think that was a turning point for me mentally. I can't tell you how sad that made me. Sam was always an inside dog, and to see him staring at me through the window almost killed me. But we needed to turn a profit, and Sam had a beautiful porch with a big doghouse. It didn't matter to him. He just wanted us.

I began making salsa. "Would you like to try a free sample of salsa?" I asked almost everyone who passed my table at the farmers market. Most people who tried it bought it. The vendors reacted with some skepticism at my tactics, but soon my sales went up and I became lovingly known as "The Salsa Lady."

After a few weeks, because of confusion as to if I could safely make the salsa, I stopped going to the market for a week. Soon I got a call from a local store on Main Street who had the booth next to me. "Why aren't you coming?" she asked.

"I'm not sure it is okay to cook in my kitchen," I responded.

"I've got a commercial kitchen! Come on over here!" the owner said. They became my friends, too.

A few weeks later, a woman from the Department of Agriculture visited me and told me I was approved to make the salsa at home as long as I kept an extra refrigerator in my home.

GOD'S GIFTS

I've got to take you on a detour, friend. Even though the seeds of discouragement had settled in my heart, the Lord still encouraged me by showing me His involvement in my life.

Let me give you a couple of examples.

After I met with the food safety lady, I knew we needed a refrigerator. The trouble was, we really didn't have any extra money for it, especially since we hadn't made any money to speak of. We constantly had to buy farm stuff just to keep up.

We checked the local used appliance place and came up empty handed. "What are we going to do about a refrigerator, Tom?"

"Maybe we should just buy a new one at Lowe's."

I thought for a few minutes. "Let me call my farm friend Kelly. She has a lot of freezers and refrigerators. Maybe she would sell us one."

We pulled into the parking lot of Lowe's when Kelly came on the line. "Hey, Kelly, I need a refrigerator for salsa. Do you have any for sale?"

"No." My heart sank. "But I do have one I'll give you!"

We pulled out of the parking lot and trekked to Kelly and Michael's place. After loading a very nice refrigerator, we thanked our friends, thanked the Lord, and smiled all the way home.

Another time, we were on our way to Wednesday night service. Our topic of discussion centered on mulch. We needed a lot of it for our plants.

"I've tried calling the big tree cutting company. They told me I just have to find a truck and see if they will come to the house," I told Tom.

"We need several truckloads to cover the asparagus and put between our rows, Pauline. I don't know how we're going to handle it. I wish we could afford a wood chipper. We have an unlimited supply of trees, and several trees that have fallen."

Suddenly, a local mulch truck pulled out in front of us. "Follow that truck!" I shouted.

We pulled into a business we'd been passing since living there.

The driver exited his vehicle and we almost pounced on him.

"Excuse me. We are local farmers and could sure use some mulch. Do you sell it?"

"Just go on inside the building and talk to Dwayne," the young man said.

"That's funny, I have a second cousin named Dwayne," Tom mentioned as he held the door for me.

As soon as the gentleman came out of his office, it was like a family reunion.

"You're never going to believe this," Tom's cousin said. "I just looked online at your fishing boat in Florida, and couldn't find any information about you there! How are you guys and what are you doing here?"

We talked for over an hour, made plans to have a meal together, and gave them our address to deliver as much mulch as we needed. All for free.

There were other gifts the Lord gave me. Most people wouldn't call them gifts, but I do. Now.

We'll get back to those gifts later, so hang in there.

ANOTHER PLANTING

As the spring turned into summer, we grew wearier. Still, we needed more product, and we'd made the decision to try and sell commercial. Out came our squash and zucchini seeds. Unlike the asparagus, we managed to plant 900 squash plants and 600 zucchini plants in just a few hours with the help of a handy bean planter. And we planted beans. In fact, we planted four 250' rows of beans. They planted easily, too. We smiled at our accomplishments.

Tom had about 400 tomato plants. Planting those took a lot of time, since unlike the squash and zucchini that we direct seeded, (that means we put the seed directly into the ground) the tomato plants had to be transplanted. We knelt by the plastic rows, digging holes and placing the plants gently into their new homes.

"What kind are these again?"

"Valencia," Tom replied.

"Those were so good last year. I can't wait to eat some!" I said as we continued. Four days later, all the tomatoes were planted. My feet hurt more and more. Occasionally, I experienced a really sharp pain in my right foot and my knees seemed to be permanently damaged from the asparagus planting.

Still, I looked forward to some time away. In a few weeks, I'd be going to Paris.

GROWING IN CHRIST

The seeds of doubt began to form in my mind. Doubt whether we should have moved. Doubting how I could continue working so hard. Even doubting God's goodness. I felt as if there were no end in sight. Plus, we continued to lose money. Where was all the cash the Lord was going to provide? Why was He letting us work so hard and go backward?

It is a good thing our Lord holds onto us. If it were the other way around, I'd be in bad shape. So would you, my friend.

Take the disciples. In Matthew 16:13–16, Jesus asks them who people say that He is.

When Jesus came to the region of Caesarea Philippi, he asked his disciples, "Who do people say that the Son of Man is?" "Well," they replied, "some say John the Baptist, some say Elijah, and others say Jeremiah or one of the other prophets." Then he asked them, "But who do you say I am?" Simon Peter answered, "You are the Messiah, the Son of the living God." (NLT)

A great declaration! Trouble was, when Jesus was arrested, they all bailed on Him. Peter even told a slave girl three times that he didn't know Jesus and cursed at her.

Jesus wasn't mad. He didn't dump them. After His resurrection He comforted them and taught them. He even made a special appearance to Peter.

God is not afraid of our doubts. But He is worthy of our trust.

If the disciples spent three years with Jesus and doubted His deity, you might be doubting also. It's okay. Jesus isn't mad. He loves you. He knows you are human.

Here are a few things you might try. Be honest with the Lord. He already knows anyway. Tell Him your doubts. Remember doubting Thomas? He didn't believe it was the risen Lord until he felt His hands and side. Thomas then declared, My Lord and my God!

Ask Him for help. You might pray something like this, or write out your own.

Lord, You know me. You know when I get up and when I lie down. You know the number of hairs on my head. That is what Your Word says. But I am having trouble right now. Please help me. Thank you for hearing the prayer of this doubting Thomas. Amen.

Chapter 7

HUMILITY

"You are nothing. Take it by faith." *–unknown missionary*

AN UNEXPECTED TRIP

Shortly after we moved to the farm, my daughter called to inform me that she and the other ladies of her husband's family were going to Paris for a girls' trip. "I'm happy for you, Sissy. I'm sure it will be fun."

Both Sarah and I knew we couldn't afford it. A few days later I received another call. "David and I decided we'd like to pay your way to come with us." I couldn't speak. Tears streaked down my dirty, farmer's-wife face.

"Mom, are you there?"

I cleared my throat. "Yes, Sarah, thank you." Wiping my eyes with the sleeve of my shirt, I managed to say, "I'd love to go to Paris with you!"

The call came in June of 2013 and our trip would be the following June. The day arrived.

My sisters would tag team with Mom, Tom would care for the farm and the animals, and I would travel abroad for the first time in my life.

There was a problem. My feet hurt—a lot. The Sunday before I left, a young lady found me crying in the bathroom. "What's the matter, Pauline?"

"My feet hurt so much, and I'm supposed to go to Paris this week. I don't know how I'm going to do it."

I took some medication and pushed forward. The day arrived. I flew to New York and met the others there. After a six-hour flight, we touched down in the most romantic city on earth.

Sarah plotted the trip to our Airbnb. We got a shuttle, then a bus, then the Metro, with a lot of fast walking in between. I gawked at the architecture and the people while Sarah directed us. After about an hour, she stopped at a hidden door on a quaint street, pushed in some numbers, and we entered.

Recessed lights softened the view of the exquisite fourteenth century architecture, trimmed with wooden beams. A small glass elevator stood in the middle.

Sarah looked at us. "Shall we go?"

I couldn't believe I had ten whole days, not only off work, and not only in Paris, but ten whole days to spend with my daughter. I couldn't have been happier.

Except my feet hurt.

By the next day I couldn't walk without crying. After several phone calls and a lot of praying, we opted to visit the local Pharmecie. It's kind of like a doctor and a pharmacy all in the same place. They gave me some medicine and a wheelchair, suggested I rest for a day, and sent us on the way.

The next day I did nothing but rest and read and chat. What a relief. I didn't worry about my mom, or selling stuff, or planting stuff, or harvesting stuff. After the complete day of rest, Sarah's sister-in-law pushed me around cobbled streets to shops, museums, and of course, restaurants.

Our social director had searched the Internet and perused

books to find the best sites and most exquisite dining for our money. One of the places we dined was Frenchie's Wine Bar on Rue de Nil. I ate pigeon for the first time and loved it! Tiny vegetables adorned the plate with a sauce, the recipe of which had been passed on from several generations of chefs. The food, of course, exceeded all expectations. (We went back the next night it was so delicious!)

At Musee d'Orsay we received special privileges because of my handicap. We passed through the Louvre in record time, tasted the macaroons from Pierre Herme. We also drank the world's best hot chocolate at Angelina's. Often, we simply ambled through parks and museums as if we didn't have a care in the world—and we didn't.

While traveling the subway, we were often treated to various kinds of music ranging from string quartets chanting melodious classical music, or Russian men spouting sturdy songs with great passion. Often, we'd stand and listen, while Becky (Sarah's mother-in-law, and my friend) recorded their beautiful music on her phone.

Becky and I rented a human rickshaw to a restaurant one evening because of my foot injury. The ride of our life lay in the hands of a reckless man from the Ukraine who threaded his jacked-up bicycle through the streets like a New York taxi driver and raced over sidewalks dodging pedestrians as if playing a computer game. Our daughters pursued us on foot— fearing for our safety. Finally, at about 15 mph he screeched to a halt, barely missing the front door of our destination. I cheered. The girls roared. Pollyanna Becky, who is the best sport I know and always happy, almost lost her smile.

It makes me smile just to think of it.

On our last evening together, Sarah asked, "What did you enjoy the most?"

"I loved having lunch on the third floor of our flat," Mary-Kathryn stated.

"I just loved walking the streets and watching the people. I loved the subway musicians, too," Becky added.

"What about you, Sarah?"

"Probably eating at Frenchie's," she stated while taking a polite bite of her passion fruit dessert pound cake.

Mine was a no-brainer. The last day of our trip we visited Montmartre. As we entered Sacre-Coeur, we gazed at magnificent architecture and read histories posted under elegant statues. We entered a roped-off area designated for prayer. All four of us sat in silence. Tears streamed down my face.

The next day, we said our goodbyes at the airport and journeyed home. Sarah returned to Tallahassee only to pack for Chapel Hill so her husband, David, could work on his MBA at the University of North Carolina. Becky and Mary-Kathryn returned to Tallahassee where they live, and I flew back to North Carolina. I went back to the States, back to my husband and Mom and our farm and back to real life.

I think the Lord knew I needed a few days off, both physically and mentally. He answered so many of my prayers in unexpected ways. After twelve years of caregiving, over a year of farming, the isolation and just plain hard work began to settle in. He knew what my future held, and He knew I needed a break before I went through some really dark times in my life.

CULTURE SHOCK AND SQUASH CATASTROPHE

Tom picked me up at the crowded Charlotte airport, noticing my distinct limp. "The squash are blooming, so are the zucchini. I also see a lot of flowers on the beans."

The transition from elegant Parisian culture back to the grit and grime of the farm life knocked me upside the head. Arriving home, I checked in with Mom, the caregiver, my sister, the chickens, and the dogs. Back to carrying five-gallon buckets of water and heavy feed.

Except I really couldn't. "You really should stay away from uneven ground, and wear good shoes with the inserts I've made for you," the foot doctor said matter-of-factly. Didn't he know we lived on a clay-filled, hilly home site filled with rocks?

I'd been working and sweating in cheap plastic shoes and now my feet would never be the same. I guess when I saw the doctor, I thought he'd give me a pill or some exercises and everything would be okay. But he didn't. Plus, we were several hundred dollars poorer.

And the work didn't go away. I went back to salsa, selling, seeding, and harvesting. And the squash, zucchini, and beans multiplied like rabbits.

Twice a day Tom harvested, along with a young man who helped us for the summer. Our neighbors felt sorry for us, so they helped, too.

"Hand me another bucket," our neighbor said as I passed him on the fifth row of our squash section. In one hand, I carried away one bucket filled with the good squash and another filled with squash with a bug hole or defect. About three times a week, Tom traveled to the co-op twelve miles away to deliver our vegetables. Often, he had twenty to thirty buckets worth.

The trouble was, the co-op could only take absolutely perfect specimens. And they had to be small, too.

"How many pounds did we have?" I asked Tom after his first trip.

"They don't go by pounds, they go by boxes. We sold six boxes of squash and five boxes of zucchini. I got all these back." He produced about thirteen buckets that were refused.

The chickens ate a lot of squash and zucchini.

"How are we doing on beans?" I asked.

"Brian picked one complete row. It took him about four hours and we have a bucket and a half."

I did the figuring. Since we paid Brian a good wage for hard work, and I could sell the beans for $2 a pound, and we had about twenty-five pounds, we maybe made $10 before counting our time and my gas driving to the markets.

No matter how hard Tom worked, he couldn't keep up. A few weeks later, he came inside about lunchtime covered with dirt and said, "I just ripped up 800 plants. I can't stand it anymore."

We let the beans fall to the ground as our tomatoes began to come in. We lost about eight of ten tomatoes from every tomato plant to bottom rot and bugs. I picked every day, along with the basil that we'd planted with it. When I looked at those rows, it made me want to cry.

Japanese beetles had also invaded. They swarmed around the basil and chewed through the tomatoes.

Another failure.

MORE CRITTERS

"When will the fencing be ready?" I asked Tom.

"It's finished! You want to see?"

Did I want to see our new pig fence? I mean, if you've seen one pig fence, you've seen them all, right? "Sure, let's go!" I said cheerily. Truth be told, I had never seen one.

We drove over to the other side of our property across and down from the old farmhouse. Constructing a 24' by 24' fence strong enough to keep hogs in had kept Tom busy for a few days. Of course, there had to be a strand of electric fence added to secure our newly acquired livestock.

"I cut apart a fifty-five-gallon plastic barrel lengthwise, and we can use them as feeders and a waterer. I also used the old corn shack in the woods, pried the bottom off and added a little wood reinforcements to give them shelter, plus a sturdy gate to keep them in."

"I'm impressed," and meant it. "When are the piglets arriving?"

"He's bringing them this evening."

A local farmer and our newfound friend arrived near dusk. He drove a large diesel truck with a trailer. In it he carried four pigs—three castrated males and a female. The idea was to raise them, process the males, and then breed the female.

"How do we get them in there?" I asked our friend. By the time I spoke the words he picked one up by all fours and plopped him in the fence. Soon all four settled into their new home while Tom and I watched. At first the tiny piglets lay down in the grass. We were unable to see them they were so small.

We would make the trek over to the chickens, feed and water them, take care of Molly and Lacey who still lived next to the hens, and then cross the dirt road to take care of the pigs.

At first, they weighed about fifty pounds and were cute, but within a few weeks they began to put on weight and their cuteness magically disappeared. Our fields held loads of overgrown squash, zucchini, and bug-eaten broccoli that the pigs loved. We used commercial feed, but all through their first few months they lived off of our discarded vegetables.

In the winter, we had no choice but to use the feed. The water and feed buckets lasted for a short time, especially as the hogs and sow grew. They stood in the feed bins and upset the water. Tom devised a watering system out of another fifty-five-gallon drum and tried securing the feeding troughs to the fence. Often, they would flip the trough or tear it from the fence. Mostly Tom kept up with them.

Their grassy enclosure soon turned to mud. Tom would venture in with them in order to refasten the feed trough or unplug the water. The pigs would nudge him and push against him when he entered. When we approached them with feed, they came running, pushing their piggy faces in the air, exposing their teeth while they drooled.

I stayed away from the pigs. We had four more mouths to feed, but hopefully they would feed us one day, and we would have more to take to market.

SHOVELING CHICKEN MANURE

"The chicken coop needs cleaning out, Pauline. We need the manure for fertilizer. I need to prune tomatoes and work on our weed takeover." Didn't he know I'd just traveled abroad? I mean, I'd just been to Paris. Now I was supposed to shovel chicken poop?

Besides, cleaning the coop wasn't my idea of a fun afternoon—I thought of whining, but I was the one who wanted chickens. Plus, everyone knows there's no whining in farming. The ladies weren't laying because of the intense heat and molting, which made me quite bitter toward them. But I resigned myself to the task.

I grabbed the manure shovel and began my chore. We mixed mulch into the coop about every other week to break down the manure, so the job began easily. As my shovel got closer to the wood bottom, the manure had hardened and shoveling became much more difficult. It didn't help that the temperature inside the coop measured about 10 degrees hotter than outside. And in mid-August, it was plenty hot outside.

I wiped sweat off my face and filled another garbage can with the material. By then I'd shoveled four cans full. After six I was ready to cry. I managed to finish and began to clean up.

"Don't forget to get the nesting boxes out and clean them."

Our nesting boxes are actually white five-gallon buckets screwed into a wood frame. As I unscrewed each bucket, I looked at my weathered hands and dirty nails.

"What am I doing here, Lord?" I cried. "In Florida, I had friends and a church and I was somebody!" Tears mixed with manure. "Here, I don't have any friends, and I'm a nobody! All people see is a middle-aged, disheveled woman selling salsa at the farmers market. Now, here I am shoveling chicken poop on the hottest day of the year all by myself."

I'd been gifted with public gifts like teaching, speaking, writing, and singing. In Florida, I'd written a few guest columns for the local newspaper whose readership numbered over one million. When the columns ran, my picture accompanied it. I thought I deserved better than shoveling chicken poop in our chicken coop, because, well, I wasn't just your average woman.

I sobbed while Tom listened to sermons in the field next to me—oblivious to my rants. That day marked a turning point for me. Looking back, it makes me think of a story my pastor in Florida used to tell about a veteran missionary retiring and being replaced by a young missionary. The young missionary asks the veteran missionary to pray for him that he would be nothing.

The veteran missionary wisely responded, "You are nothing. Take it by faith."

I had just finished studying John chapters 12 and 13. Two stories stuck out to me. One concerned Mary anointing Christ with the costly perfume. She displayed sacrificial love and amazing tenderness. Right after that, Jesus took a towel and washed the disciples' feet—even the feet of His betrayer, Judas. Then He said something earth-shaking, "Do you know what I have done to you? You call Me Teacher and Lord; and you are right, for *so* I am. If I then, the Lord and the Teacher, washed your feet, you also ought to wash one another's feet" (John 13:12b–14).

The characteristic those two stories have in common is humility. The teacher of the study I'm in said, "Know your position—on the ground."

GROWING IN CHRIST

I didn't know my position.

But the Lord was going to show me. Just like our plants needed pruning and fertilizing, to be useful to Him, He knew I needed a little manure shoveling and cutting away at my pride in order to know my position.

Proverbs 14:4 states, "Without oxen a stable stays clean, but you need a strong ox for a large harvest" (NLT).

So what? you may ask. Let me give you the Pauline Hylton translation…in order for you to get eggs, there will be chicken poop. And before there is spiritual growth, there must be humility.

And I needed lots of it…still do.

The Bible talks a lot about humility. The book of Proverbs is chocked full of it. Take a look at these:

"When pride comes, then comes disgrace, but with humility comes wisdom" (Prov. 11:2 NIV).

"Pride brings a person low, but the lowly in spirit gain honor" (Proverbs 29:23 NIV).

"Humility is the fear of the Lord; its wages are riches and honor and life" (Prov. 22:4 NIV).

And don't get me started on humility in the New Testament. The Beatitudes give a great start, and Philippians 2:6–8 knocks it out of the park.

"Though he was God, he did not think of equality with God as something to cling to. Instead, he gave up his divine privileges; he took the humble position of a slave and was born as a human being. When he appeared in human form, he humbled himself in obedience to God and died a criminal's death on a cross" (NLT).

Shoveling chicken manure became a wake-up call to my pride.

What about you? Is your pride getting in the way of your spiritual growth? Don't let it, my friend. "God opposes the proud but favors the humble" (James 4:6 NLT).

True humility is kind of a contrast. On one hand, we see ourselves as a sinful creature in front of our marvelous, holy Creator. It causes us to fall on our knees and cry out like Isaiah, "It's all over! I am doomed, for I am a sinful man. I have filthy lips, and I live among a people with filthy lips. Yet I have seen the King, the LORD of Heaven's Armies" (Isaiah 6:5 NLT).

On the other hand, we understand we are now children of God. Redeemed. Loved. Cherished. Ephesians 3:18 says this, "And may you have the power to understand, as all God's people should, how wide, how long, how high, and how deep his love is" (NLT).

His love for us humbles us as it should.

Make no mistake, humility is necessary for salvation and spiritual growth.

I know I keep saying this, but ask the Lord to show you your pride. He will. And just like surgery, it's painful, but it is also healing.

Chapter 8

ISOLATION

"No man is an island, entire of itself." — John Donne

CAREGIVING AND CRYING

After being trapped in our house for two weeks from a big snow in a place where supposedly it never snows, I experienced not only isolation but also claustrophobia. Mom's caregiver made it a few days since she had four-wheel drive, but I couldn't get out of our 900' driveway.

Tom researched his heart out, which made him as happy as a clam. (Although I don't know why clams are so happy; perhaps they have the Internet in their shells.)

Let me tell you a little bit about my mental state of mind and maybe you can relate.

Caregiving up to this point involved my parents moving in with our family of four in 2002 when my kids still needed me, Dad losing both legs to diabetes, role reversals for my parents, and then role reversals for me. Oftentimes I felt as if I were the man at the circus, spinning plates. I'd get one life plate spinning and another would begin to fall. Rushing over to steady that one, the other crashed.

103

I kept the parent plates moving pretty well—doctor appointments, emergency visits to the hospital, keeping track of medications—the list seemed endless. Meanwhile, my teenagers' plates fell and Tom's wobbled. He kept busy running our charter fishing business, and we attempted to have regular date nights, but often my caregiving responsibilities took precedence.

There came a time when I had what hospice deemed caregiver breakdown. Overwhelmed became the norm for me, and many of my friends were afraid for my health. My daughter had a life-changing experience that changed our lives, too. She needed me and I was too busy with my parents.

Tom and I made some hard choices by readjusting our priorities. I distanced myself from my parents emotionally to protect my sanity and save energy for my kids. I became very good at maintaining that distance as a caregiver. If not, I would be overwhelmed with sadness.

During that long winter, I felt myself edging closer to that caregiver breakdown place again, and it scared me. During one of those snowy days on the farm after Mom called me into her room five times within a couple of hours, instead of showing love and compassion, I snapped at her.

"Mom, I can't come in here every time you call!" Then my sweet mother began to cry and so did I. Escaping from her room I fell on my bed and sobbed.

Then I called my sister. "Paulette, I just yelled at Mom and I feel terrible! She's crying and I can't stop!"

My sister has the uncommon ability to make everyone feel special. Often, I'd called her during Dad's long illness, and she knew just what to say. Plus, she always prayed with me. This time was no different.

A little while later, Mom called me into her room. Ashamed, I entered.

"I'm sorry I made you feel bad, Pauline," she said after much crying, sniffing, and wiping of eyes.

"I'm sorry, too, Mom." I grabbed a tissue, blew my nose and placed the dirty one on her tray along with several others. "Sometimes I just need time alone so I don't go crazy."

"I know," she said, patting my hand. Tom knew there'd been a problem and came in. And just like my sister, he prayed. And we all hugged and then watched another *NCIS* rerun.

Back then caregiving was a duty. I knew it. Unfortunately, I think Mom knew it and the Lord knew it.

And He was going to change it.

THE BIG BUILDING PROJECT

Don arrived from Milwaukee one evening in early February. We hardly knew him. I'd met him on several occasions. His wife and my sister Paula were best friends, so they both came to many family events. When he heard of the grant we'd been given to build a commercial-sized hoop house, he volunteered to help. Retiring as a middle-school principle for the Milwaukee County School system, he told us later he had been sitting at his cabin thinking about what he could do to help someone when Colleen, his wife, told him about our situation.

What Don didn't know was that I'd been praying for someone to help Tom put up the 80' x 30' building. Don was my answer to prayer.

"You mean he's driving all the way from Milwaukee to help us?" Tom asked incredulously.

"I guess so. I hope he likes us since he's planning to be here a week."

And it was the coldest week of the year. Tom had no time for computer research because Don popped out of bed from his blow-up mattress at six a.m. ready to work. Tom resisted. Born and raised in Florida, 3 degrees above zero and snowing wasn't exactly hoop house building weather.

They worked tirelessly for a week. They planned, chatted, argued, and constructed for eight hours a day. One day I drove past the field and observed Tom raising Don up into the air about twelve feet on the front loader of the tractor, connecting something at the tip-top of the hoop house. I prayed he wouldn't fall.

Each evening we cooked dinner, sat in the living room, and talked. Mom often joined us in her wheelchair. "How are you doing tonight, Mrs. Wert?" Don would ask.

He fit right into our family. When the day came for him to go, we were sad. He and Tom had finished the main structure, but Tom would need to do other work in order to add the last ingredient. Plastic. Utilizing several tennis balls, they would need to throw the plastic over the top and then secure it.

"I'll come back when you're ready to throw the tennis balls over," Don said, smiling and waving as he drove away.

And he did. My sister Paula came, too. Phones ready, we recorded the initial tennis balls over the top of the twenty-plus foot metal framework as we whooped (no pun intended) and hollered and high-fived.

Don and Paula were gifts from the Lord sent to encourage me in my isolation. But it hit hard when they left.

LOSING THE ROMANCE

Early in our marriage, I'd read an article about an in-house date night and decided to try it. We tried to be diligent to keep one night just for ourselves from the time our kids were in grade school all the way through high school. In fact, one date night evening, our children were out so we posted a sign on the front door that read, Date night. Mom and Dad on back porch. Do not disturb. We pulled the blinds, and climbed in the Jacuzzi on our back porch to relax.

Soon, we heard a commotion in the room by the back porch. Our thirteen-year-old son arrived home with his friend.

Friend: Where are your parents?

Micah: They're on the back porch. It's date night.

Friend: Let's go out and say hello.

Micah shouting: No! (grabs friend by shirt) Trust me, it will scar you for life!

Since farming, our date nights were few and far between. At first, it was because we worked sixteen-hour days and could barely speak by the end of the evening. Add to that working together 24/7 definitely put a strain on our relationship.

Then there was my isolation and depression. It grew to the point I found it difficult to even be around other people. Tom seemed so happy. He did what he loved, served at church, and continued to learn about various methods of farming.

I felt like no one locally really knew me. Or liked me— except Mom and she had no choice. The stress of farming, selling, marketing, finances began to weigh so heavily on my heart it affected our marriage.

I began to distance myself from Tom, too. And that's not a good place to be.

GETTING BUSY

February turned to March. Mom's health declined, but if we were going to make a living at this, we had no time to waste. Choosing seeds and starting plants became our regimen. Tom started several varieties of tomatoes, along with eggplant, peppers, and greens. I continued to work in my kitchen to make jellies, pesto, and salsa, but it proved more and more difficult.

We had a few vegetables plus all the products I made when the market opened in April. The trouble was, our caregiver got sick. Now when your child gets sick, you can have a friend, or relative, or even a babysitter come by. But when you are caregiving, it takes a special person to do that.

After a few days, I found a woman to help during that week, but it put us at a disadvantage. I didn't want to leave the new lady for very long at first, so I limited myself to working out in the fields or short trips to town.

We were able to attend the first market in Dobson together, although we drove separately. We didn't expect to make much, which we didn't, but some money is still money, and we traveled home a little richer.

Until I got a text from Tom that read, At vet, found puppy. You'll be impressed.

I met him at the vet's office. In his arms, he cradled a tiny brown and black bundle. "I was driving down Johnson Road when he ran across the road. I got out of the car and called, and he came. Look at this," he said pointing to his back paw. "It looks like he had barbed wire wrapped around it and couldn't get out."

The paw appeared twisted and bloody. An hour later, after we spent half of what we made at the market, we took our new puppy to his forever home at Peeled Poplar Farm.

We'd forgotten how much work a new puppy could be. And this one proved an exceptional amount of work. We fashioned a pen for him on the front porch, put in a radio, food, and water. After playing with him for several hours, we attempted to put him to bed. He howled all night. Since he and Sam shared the front porch, Sam didn't sleep either.

We hadn't named him yet. "How about Luke?" I asked. Tom shook his head. He Googled dog names.

After an hour or so of possible names, I said, "How about we name him after the dog in the Mitford Series, who is named after Barnabas in the book of Acts? It means son of encouragement." The howling puppy with the bum foot became our beloved Barnabas.

A few days later I thought I heard an echo of his howl in the woods. Instead, a beautiful little husky mix appeared in our yard and all of a sudden—including Molly and Lacey, we owned five dogs and two cats. Another cat joined our family one evening, wandering out of the woods, emaciated, yellow fur tangled and matted. We named him Bree, after the talking horse in *The Chronicles of Narnia*.

More mouths to feed. But they were cute mouths.

PET DRAMA

If we thought we were busy before the dogs and extra cat arrived, we were mistaken. Not only did they consume our time, but our money, too. Both dogs needed vet visits and shots. Of course, they'd need collars. And both cats and dogs required flea, tic, and heartworm medicine. It cost more for them to live than us—and they were not part of our budget.

A few days after the new puppy arrived, we named him Cooper. Sitting at our dining room table with Mom one day, I glanced out the window. Bree hurtled himself through the air, capturing a male redbird in his mouth. I raced out of the house, grabbed Bree by the scruff of the neck and shook him with all my might. "Drop him, Bree!"

No way was he letting go of his prey. I resorted to prying his jaw open and freeing the frightened bird. His mate watched in horror from a nearby tree. The male fell to the ground, stunned by the attack. Before I could retrieve him to set him free, Cooper gobbled him up. With about four bites, the bird disappeared forever—my turn to be stunned.

What kind of wild puppies do we own?

But each evening, when we finished our farm work, we let the puppies and kittens out in the yard while we sat in the grass. Eventually, they would push us down, climb on our chests, and lick our faces.

When I tucked my children into bed each night, I would ask them, "What was your favorite part of the day?" The answers varied from swimming to playing with friends or visiting Grandma and Grandpa. If anyone would have asked me that question, hands down the answer involved those puppies and kittens licking our faces. I think it's one of the best feelings in the world.

What I didn't love was chasing them. If we weren't farming or caring for Mom, we were chasing puppies. One minute, they were right next to us in the yard, the next minute they disappeared, often with Sam accompanying them. No kidding, I think we spent fifteen hours a week trying to find them. It's not that we didn't confine them, they just seemed to know how to sneak away.

After one long day looking for them, all three of them came ramping up about a half a mile away from the pasture in front of our house—Sam in the lead, Cooper close behind him, with Barnabas limping along in the rear. It played like a scene from *Homeward Bound*. We tried scolding them, but couldn't. Tails wagging, mouths drooling, we were glad to have them home.

At first, Barnabas did not live up to his name. When we called, he ran, when we grabbed him, he nipped. Tom almost cursed the day he rescued him.

Near the end of May, I took the puppies for their last shots. After returning, I kissed Tom goodbye, pet the dogs, rubbed the cats, and climbed back in the car.

I drove with Sarah to Tallahassee for a baby shower celebrating her unborn baby boy. Shortly after leaving, Tom called. "Cooper doesn't look good. He's under the porch and won't eat."

"Probably just the shots," I assured him. I received another call from him a few days later. Cooper still wouldn't eat. By Sunday, he wasn't drinking.

Sarah and I traveled home on Memorial Day. "He died, Pauline. I tried feeding him rice and giving him water. But he just got weaker. I even called the vet but no one is on duty since it's a holiday. I'd have to go to Winston to a vet we don't know."

I noticed a catch in Tom's voice. I cried. "I buried him with his collar over by the edge of the yard. This has been hard."

I know in farming, there are casualties, but death is difficult, especially with a pet. I arrived home to bad Barnabas barking, and Sam jumping. Bree, Reep, and Cheep rubbed up against my leg. I took my time with each one—petting, rubbing, scratching their ears. Hiking to the chickens, I hugged Molly and Lacey and told them what good girls they were. But I noticed we were one tail short.

And it hurt.

MORE DOG DRAMA

We'd settled into our sixteen-hour-a-day summer routine with chickens laying and vegetables exploding. One evening when we headed over to the chickens, we decided to take our dogs with us.

"Load up, Sam. Come on, Barnabas," Tom said, opening the tailgate to the back of our pickup.

We pulled out and onto the dirt road to the other side of our property where the chickens ranged. Hearing a thump, I glanced out the side mirror. Barnabas lay on the ground, unable to move. "Tom, stop! It's Barnabas!"

We rushed out of the truck to find our puppy sprawled on

the road, whimpering. Tom scooped him up and we headed to the vet…again.

"It looks like he may have broken this back leg, but I'd need to x-ray it. The front paw appears to have nerve damage, but again, I'm not sure. Leave him tonight, and I'll get back with you in the morning," the vet said.

Neither of us spoke on the way home. A deep pit rested in our stomachs. Our hearts hurt. Our bodies ached. It didn't seem like we did anything right.

The next day we picked him up and paid the very high vet bill. "Keep him sedated and confined for several weeks," the tech stated, handing us three bottles of pills. "We'll have to see how that right front paw comes along since there is nerve damage. He'll either accommodate, or if it gets infected, we may have to amputate." She looked at our worn faces. "I'm sorry."

We were too.

Again, we placed Barnabas in the makeshift pen on the front porch while Sam looked on. "It will be hard to keep him quiet, Pauline, but we've got to try." And we did. Over the next four weeks, we carried him off the porch to use the bathroom, spent time petting him, administered medicine, and prayed.

Eventually, he could get down the porch steps and play with Sam—whether Sam wanted to or not. He chased Bree again, placing Bree's whole head in his mouth (which the cat loved).

Soon, Barnabas seemed to be back to normal—except his right front paw didn't work. He'd flop it out in front of him and shuffle along. His back leg was better, but he still walked with a limp, and at any given time it seemed to slip out of the socket.

In spite of the mangled back paw, his broken back leg, and nerve-dead front paw, Barnabas wagged his tail constantly. The mischievous puppy named for the Son of Encouragement, became an encouragement to me.

SALSA, SALES, AND STRESS

The markets moved along, ebbing and flowing like the tide. One week I'd make $500 and another week it would be $300. My chickens laid eggs but so did everyone else's. Salsa and pesto continued to be our best seller so each week making those two value-added products always appeared on my list. Not only that, all of our vegetables ripened at once. I needed to process them into either salsa, pesto, jellies, or freeze them to use later. A lot of our harvest went straight to the pigs or chickens. There simply weren't enough hours in the day to do it all.

I tried to keep my restaurant contacts up to date, but often my products were sporadic. I cannot impress on you enough how overwhelmed and incompetent I felt. All. The. Time.

Along with my farm concerns, my caregiving responsibilities played like elevator music in the back of my mind. As soon as I walked in the door, I checked on Mom. I knew the caregivers took good care of her, but she wanted me. She needed me so much and because of the worry, work, and isolation, I avoided her. It was too painful. There wasn't any me left.

After the caregivers left in the evening, I'd go in and watch a little TV with her. We rarely talked. In fact, Mom's ability to carry on a conversation took a nosedive. While sitting in her wheelchair her body leaned all the way over to one side—just like my dad did the last year of his life. I'd get her snack, clean her up, sing with her, and kiss her goodnight.

And fall into bed, usually without much sleep.

SILAS

"After Silas is born, can you come and stay for a week?" Sarah asked.

"Sure!" I said, wondering if I could cover the caregiving responsibilities with Mom. Plus, I wasn't sure if I knew how to be a grandma. There were a few reasons for that.

When I was a teenager, I babysat for a young couple down the street who had a newborn. I woke up when they entered for the evening. Needless to say, they never hired me again. And then there was the time I watched a little girl who locked me in a closet. But the main reason I doubted my grandma credit score was the egg game.

You see, when I worked with underprivileged girls in Florida, we played a game called Watch the Egg. The leaders gave each girl a hard-boiled egg and a cheap plastic basket filled with Easter grass. Their task—to watch the egg for an entire week without leaving it.

I flunked. Left it at a restaurant. When my friend Pam, the co-leader, found out I was pregnant with Sarah, instead of congratulating me, she exclaimed, "Oh no!"

With a lot of prayer and God's grace, I managed to keep my kids alive, but could I handle a grandson? Would he even like me?

Because of a few complications, Tom and I ended up taking two weeks off from both the market and farming. That would cost us a lot, but how often do you have a first grandchild? The ripened vegetables would either have to wait or rot.

Finally, on August 10, we sat with Sarah's in-laws, the Healys, and drank coffee in the outdoor café of the University of North Carolina hospital. At about six p.m. we were summoned.

My baby and her husband held their baby, and all four grandparents met David Silas Healy—Silas. We marveled at his tiny hands and admired his intelligent gaze. Becky and I held him tight and whispered loving words into his perfect ears. The men passed on holding him—at least for the first night. We left satisfied.

New grandfather Dave Healy said, "That's the great thing about being a grandparent: we get to see him and then we go out to eat."

If we were football players, we would have chest bumped, but being the middle-aged grandparents that we were, we shook hands, hugged, and congratulated ourselves.

The next day everyone left but me. I accompanied the new family home in the car and helped while Sarah and David adjusted to their new charge. I'd forgotten how much work babies were. I did enjoy being with them. I cleaned, cooked, did laundry, held Silas, and began to tell him about his family—usually in song. One day, Sarah picked David up from work and left me alone with my grandson. I composed and performed a twenty-minute ballad about the Hylton family dogs while we both lay on the floor. He stared at me with his soulful eyes.

"Did you love him right away, Mom?" Sarah asked a few days later?

The question startled me. Not being the doting Nana, (that's my name) and leery of most children, I responded, "Sarah, at first, I loved him because you love him. I didn't know him, yet." She looked concerned. "But now I do," I said, hugging my grandson.

Sarah didn't want me to leave after a week. I didn't want to leave either because when I arrived home, I would again carry the weight of Mom's care and the farm. Taking care of someone else's responsibility is much easier.

Plus, Silas was pretty cute…and light.

GROWING IN CHRIST

Isolation can be both good and bad. For instance, take the apostle Paul. He spent three years in Arabia after his conversion. Our Lord went away for forty days in the desert and often took long periods of time to spend in solitude while on this earth. Sometimes, we need to step away from our busy lives to think and pray. That's good.

Isolation is harmful when you distance yourself from the body of Christ. Talking can be painful, and you sure don't want anyone to ask hard questions. They may find out your marriage isn't perfect, or your teenager is on drugs, or your bank account is empty.

Those are exactly the times you need your spiritual family. Listen to this passage from 1 Corinthians 12:12–13. "The human body has many parts, but the many parts make up one whole body. So it is with the body of Christ. Some of us are Jews, some are Gentiles, some are slaves, and some are free. But we have all been baptized into one body by one Spirit, and we all share the same Spirit." Verse 26 goes on to say, "If one part suffers, all the parts suffer with it, and if one part is honored, all the parts are glad" (NLT).

The church—His body here on earth—is made up of all kinds of people with all kinds of problems. We need to be there for each other.

Don't isolate yourself, my friend. Unless you are getting away to be with the Lord, isolation can be dangerous and definitely unhealthy for a follower of Christ. Reach out. Make that phone call. Get dressed and go to church. It might be uncomfortable, but you may be comforted.

If you cannot be honest with the people at your church, find a different one. Email me. Call someone you trust. Ask the Lord.

Chapter 9

DESPAIR

"Why are you in despair, O my soul? And why have you become disturbed within me? Hope in God, for I shall again praise Him For the help of His presence." Psalm 42:5

AN UNEXPECTED GIFT AND BELOVED VISITORS

S o, the plan is to sell everything and RV around until we find a place that is suitable for Geoff and his allergies. He can work from home. We sold our home in Clearwater, bought our new home on wheels, and a monster truck," my young friend from Florida said.

"Wow. That's quite a change. When are you leaving?" I couldn't believe that my city-goer friends were branching out into RV world—to roam the country, no less!

"About two weeks."

I'd called Keri-Rose to ask her if she knew anyone who had a car for sale. Our van wouldn't last much longer, and we wanted to check with friends and family in case they knew of anything. She'd surprised me with the information of their new adventure.

"What are you looking for in a car?" she asked.

"Since everywhere we need to go is about ten miles, we'd love a car that's good on gas."

"Let me get back to you," she said.

A few days later, she called. "Geoff and I would like you to have our Scion. You remember it. It's gray and gets between 32-35 mpg."

"How much do you want for it?" I vaguely remembered their car.

"Nothing. We don't need it and you do."

That conversation sent Tom and I to Florida for a day in late August to pick up a car from our brother and sister in Christ. It's funny, I give stuff away a lot and hardly ever have second thoughts about it. Before we moved from Florida, I gave this young friend a vegetable cutter worth about $70. A few times I'd thought about it and wished I had kept it. Now, they shared a car with us worth about $5000. God's economy is so much better than ours.

An added benefit was they would begin their journey at an RV park about five miles up the road from us. "We think we'll stay for a month."

I was so lonely and depressed; their visit was even a better gift than the car.

THE BLACK HOLE

Keri-Rose sat at our wooden table as her eighteen-month-old ran around our living room. Mom sat with us and stared blankly at little Levi as she leaned heavily to one side.

"You want some lunch, Mom?" Slowly her gaze traveled to me. She nodded imperceptibly. Mashed vegetables and soft meat filled a tiny plate. I placed a fork in her hands as she slowly stabbed at food. Eventually, I knew she would need help, but still my desire was for her to do as much as she could.

Which wasn't much.

In a few days, we'd celebrate her ninety-fifth birthday. Not bad for a woman who at the young age of twenty-one was told she had a serious heart problem and would probably die. I'd say the Lord had different plans.

Her declining health became more evident each day and difficult for me to bear.

Keri-Rose and I caught up on all our news while Mom tried to push food to her fork and, with an extreme amount of concentration, bring the fork to her mouth. Some food made it, but most didn't. It was time to put Mom in bed for her nap.

After Mom was safely tucked in, I joined my friend in the kitchen. I couldn't stop crying. It seemed to be a pattern for the last few weeks. K-Ro (that's what I call her) has her masters in social work. She listened carefully and asked thoughtful questions. Just having someone I knew loved me sit across the table from me and listen meant so much. But I couldn't shake my depression.

Mom's main caregiver became sick again. Tom thought we needed to make major changes in Mom's caregiving team. We switched to a local hospice and gave the majority of the new hours to a caregiver that only worked part time up to that point. The trouble was she'd just had surgery, so I became Mom's full-time caregiver for a while, during the caregiver's recuperation period. Those silent weeks seemed to drag on for me, adding to my isolation and despair. Even having my grandson close didn't raise my spirits.

A few weeks after Mom's birthday, my sisters and my daughter, Sarah, traveled to our farm to celebrate. We set up a long table on our front porch, punched holes in white plastic trash bags and used them for bibs for all-we-could-eat crab legs. Paula's friend Colleen celebrated with us, along with Sarah, Sarah's friend from Florida, and their babies. Silas lay in my arms as we dined. When I think back on that night, it still makes me smile.

A few days later Paula and Paulette took me to lunch. We

sat in a lodge-like restaurant in Winston-Salem. "Pauline, we are concerned about you and worried about your health. I don't want caregiving for our mother to make you sick," my oldest sister, Paula, said.

Paulette looked at me. "Pauline, you've been a trooper this far, and if you need to stop, I understand. It's up to you."

Embarrassed because of my many tears in a public place, I barely whispered, "I don't want to give up," I blew my nose and sobbed out, "because I might miss a blessing."

I knew that the Lord often used difficulty to bring blessing. What is truly good is usually hard. Caregiving was a marathon, and I didn't want to quit at the last mile marker.

And so, it was decided. Mom would stay with us until the end. And the end was nearer than I thought.

A LITTLE JOY

Newborn Silas lay in his car seat on top of our dining room table. Mom watched him intently.

"Is he warm enough?" she said clearly.

"I think so, Mom." Sarah and Tom traveled into town for a little daddy-daughter time while I stayed home with my mother and new grandson. I fed Mom and watched over Silas. I couldn't believe the responsibility I felt. Yet, I enjoyed seeing Mom admire her great-grandson.

Mom's face crinkled. "Are you sure he's warm enough?" she asked for the fifth time.

"I don't know. I'm new at this, too."

Sarah visited in mid-September since David spent sixteen hours a day in school. While she stayed with us, K-Ro, Levi, Sarah, Silas, and I visited an apple orchard in Virginia. On the way back, I sang a fifty-minute rendition of the ABC song to squelch crying and complaining. Really, we had a grand time and even came home with a few bushels of apples that we picked.

In the evenings, we'd use a hydraulic machine to lift Mom out of her wheelchair and place her in the big leather chair right by our new wood stove. In order to fit the legs of the hydraulic lift under the leather chair, we bought items that fit under each leg and elevated the chair about four inches off the floor. Placing Silas in her arms for short periods of time brought us all much joy.

During that time, I often thought of the famous passage in Ecclesiastes about a time to be born and a time to die. Mom and Silas were at opposite ends of the spectrum. Mom became more and more dependent, while as Silas grew, he'd grow more and more independent.

I knew all of these things were normal, but there is something stark about it when viewed up close.

Each week the Lanottes were in the area, (K-Ro, Geoff, and Levi) they joined us for dinner a couple of times a week. It was always a treat. Once, Geoff even scheduled himself to help Tom with the farmers market.

"Geoff's not here yet, Tom. That's unusual. He's usually early," I remarked.

Soon we received a phone call from 6'7" Geoff. "I don't know what to do. I'm a few houses away from you but am surrounded by little white dogs! I don't want to run over them."

We roared. Three white dogs stood guard on Johnson Road and when the notion struck them, they chased cars. We'd learned that you just had to keep driving, or they'd win.

Geoff didn't know that so Tom rescued him. He found Geoff surrounded by three white mutts yipping hard. Tom chased them away and off they went to the market.

Saying goodbye to Geoff, K-Ro, and Levi proved difficult.

We'd enjoyed our time of friendship and fellowship, but while our adventure became more difficult, their adventure was just beginning. Their last night with us proved to be special. Especially since they told us there would be a fourth member of their family due in May.

MAKING SALSA

"How many salsas are we going to make today, Pauline?" the caregiver asked.

"I have two boxes of tomatoes, so we should make about sixty-eight or so. Last week in Elkin I sold almost fifty. I think that is the most I've sold there so far."

I'd also begun to make a pinot grigio jelly infused with herbs from our kitchen garden. People seemed to really like it and no one else had a white wine jelly—especially made with herbs. I even left a sprig of herb in the jar that made the product more enticing.

That next week I only sold about twenty-eight salsas total. I couldn't believe it! Nearing the end of August, it was still very hot, and only a few salsa buyers? The next week was worse. Although we had a few heirloom tomatoes and a lot of peppers, I hardly sold anything at the market.

In any given week, I'd have a few extra salsas. I'd usually give them to friends or have someone over, but I began to have thirty to forty left over. I cut down on the amount I processed and still had leftover. Not wanting to completely stop making it since it was our biggest moneymaker, I continued. I ended up feeding salsa to the chickens.

And the hen union must have called a strike because they weren't laying. At all. The rub was I still had to feed and water them twice a day. And their feed wasn't cheap.

We continued to have a mega-squash harvest with base-ball-bat-sized zucchini. Finally, I ended up giving loads to a few local restaurants and bushels of it to the Salvation Army. A lot of produce rotted in the fields. It couldn't be helped.

Our work on the farm didn't decrease, if anything, it increased. Each morning we got up with a list a mile long, my stomach churning. Each evening we worked outside until dark and then went inside to work on other projects.

There was no time to sit on the porch or play with Sam or the kittens. No time for baseball games on the tiny TV in Mom's room. No time for each other. And when we were together, we talked about the farm and often disagreed on how to proceed.

To top things off, Mom's health declined significantly. I worried about that. In fact, worry became my constant companion.

How are we ever going to make a living at this? What is going to happen to Mom? Will I ever be able to take off to see my children or have any friends?

ANOTHER CATASTROPHE

In October, I resumed some farm chores as the caregiver came back full time. I had tried to apply for jobs a few months earlier, but realized before Mom was "promoted to glory," I needed to be available.

One day while feeding the chickens, I noticed Lacey didn't get up to meet me, which was unusual. I visited her in the dog-house and noticed a general lack of energy.

"How are you, girl?" She looked at me but had no sparkle in her eyes.

I told Tom about it that night. "Lacey looks sick. I don't see anything wrong with her, but she didn't get up to meet me."

"Are you sure she didn't have a fight with Molly?" Tom

asked. Often the two dogs got into very loud violent fights. I didn't blame them. Living with chickens was not only boring, but highly annoying. "We'll check on her tomorrow."

The next day she was much worse. "I think we better take her in, Pauline," Tom said. So once again Tom scooped a sick dog into his arms for a trip to the vet.

"Frankly, I don't know what's wrong with her," the vet said. "Let me call you later after I do some tests."

We went home and waited. After a phone call, they still weren't sure, and we agreed to a few more tests. The next morning, we received a call.

"Mrs. Hylton, I'm sorry to tell you that Lacey passed away during the night." She paused. "We are so sorry. It was probably a birth defect since her kidneys failed. Would you like us to take care of her body?"

I couldn't handle any more sadness, and Tom had already buried one puppy. "Yes, please just take care of it." So just like that, we lost another dog along with several hundred dollars. I didn't know how much more I could take.

I didn't care about anything—if I lived or died—if I stayed married or not. All I knew was there was a big pit in my stomach all the time and I had no joy.

Then Barnabas ran away. He'd been sneaking off with a rogue group of dogs for a while. These dogs resembled the scary ones in bad cartoons. But once I met them, I petted them, and they spent an afternoon on my porch.

After that, my two cats Reep and Cheep disappeared never to be seen again. Think they moved to a better home?

No matter what we did, we couldn't get Barnabas to stay home. The underground electric fence didn't work on him, so we basically gave up. He began to disappear overnight. Often when Tom would check his deer camera, he'd see Barnabas romping through the woods at two a.m.

He usually just left for the day, but sometimes he would take off for a day or two. One day he didn't come home.

"Tom, Barnabas has been gone a few days. Do you think he's all right?"

"I don't know, but there is nothing we can do about it."

I did do something, though. I visited the trailer through the woods. Barnabas often stayed at their place with kids and other dogs to play with.

"Have you seen our dog Barnabas?" I asked. "He's black and brown and has a limp."

"Oh, you mean Skittles? That's what we call him."

It figures. Barnabas leads a double life.

"No, I haven't seen him. In fact, we're missing our white dog. Been gone about five days."

"That's the same time Barnabas has been gone." We exchanged phone numbers and promised to call if either one of us heard anything.

After he'd been gone a week, I got down on my knees and prayed. "Lord, I know Barnabas is a pain-in-the-neck, but so am I. I miss him, Lord. Please, would you please send him home?" I wiped my eyes and blew my nose and went on with my day.

The next day Tom chopped firewood at the edge of our yard. I heard him calling. "Pauline, come quick. Barnabas is home, but he's in bad shape."

I really couldn't have prepared myself for his appearance. Most of his fur had fallen out, he had sores on his head, under his head, and on his back. His only good leg had been bitten so hard the bone lay exposed. Blood and matted fur covered his emaciated frame.

"I'm going to throw him in the shower," Tom said.

A good while later, Tom came out with our puppy. I tried to

pet him, but I couldn't find a place he wasn't injured. It looked like a wild animal or other dog had just chewed on him until he was half dead. When would it all end?

Believe it or not, Barnabas survived. I'd called the vet's office, told them we couldn't afford anymore care for our dog, and they suggested keeping him calm and giving him an antibiotic that we happened to have left over from Mom's meds.

Soon, he wagged his tail and chased the cat again and was his usual pain-in-the-neck self. A few short weeks and it would be Christmas.

MY LACK OF FAITH

Once upon a time, I was going to write a book on faith—because I thought I had it. As time moved on through that difficult season that dark winter enlightened me to my lack of faith.

It's kind of like a ski trip our family experienced several years ago. Growing up in flat country, I'd never learned to ski. When we vacationed with friends in Steamboat Springs, Colorado, I decided to take a beginner's class.

My friend Linda ranked well above beginner, but her daughter (my daughter's best friend) took the class with me.

"Mrs. Hylton, we're supposed to join the other class members over there." Kimberly pointed to a group of happy student skiers about thirty feet away on a slight incline to my right. My brain told my feet to glide gracefully up to them. But my feet couldn't figure out how to do it since I'd have to use a side-step move with my skis.

I came face-to-face with the ground about six times, laughed like a pro several times, and swallowed about three handfuls of snow. Twenty minutes later, we arrived at our destination while the other students departed to trek the bunny hill.

Kimberly and I stumbled over to the hill and began our downhill adventure. After thirty minutes, we high-fived each other for the completion of that simple slope.

"You made it, Mrs. Hylton! We made it!"

"Of course, we did. It doesn't matter that we fell more than we skied—we finished!" We couldn't wait to tell Linda, who'd been skiing while we practiced falling.

"Linda! We finished and did the whole slope!" we chanted.

"Great!" She smiled. "How about we do this one together?" she said pulling out a placemat-sized map of the resort. She pointed to a slope about halfway up.

"Yeah! Let me show you the slope Kimberly and I skied!" Confidently, I searched the map. Finally, I lowered my eyes to the very bottom of the placemat. Our slope appeared about a quarter inch above the bottom. Our accomplishment barely registered on the ski slope map.

A few years ago, I thought my faith ranked way up on the faith-scale map, when in reality, it barely registered. Several dynamics surfaced in our family in the last months of that year that confirmed that.

First, Mom was completely bedridden. It was impossible to take her to church, so I began to stay home from church myself. Fortunately for us we were able to view my Florida church family through live stream, but it wasn't the same.

I'd get her breakfast and listen to a few TV preachers and then clean up while she napped. After I cleaned her up, I'd put her in her wheelchair and push her to the living room in front of our twenty-four inch computer monitor. We'd sing the first few hymns together and then usually Mom fell asleep. When Tom arrived home, we'd share lunch as he talked about the Sunday school class he taught and the worship service. Often, he would open his Bible and share the passage our pastor covered.

"Everyone said to say hello and that they missed you."

I missed them, too even though I hadn't really made any friends at church. I was too busy with farming, food processing, marketing, and caregiving to commit to anything else outside my family.

With hospice involved, I didn't have to worry if she had an infection or something major wrong with her. Hospice visited, administered care, and took care of all of her medications. Still, it was difficult for me to watch Mom's decline.

My isolation set in gradually. It kind of snuck up on me like wrinkles. Eventually, it would overwhelm me.

During the month of November that year, I pushed Mom out to the porch on a sunny day. My day was terrible. If I were a toddler, I would have put on my pouty face and sat on the floor with crossed arms. Ungrateful, moody, unhappy, and exhausted, I searched my brain for anything that I might be able to do well that day.

I can be a good caregiver. We stared out onto the wide-open pasture dotted with cows—Mom in her wheelchair, me in the shiny black rocker. Mom needed help in bathing, walking, and toiletry. I was my mother's mother. In fact, sometimes she even called me her mother.

I thought of a question.

I glanced over at a woman who had served the Lord faithfully for decades. "Mom, if there were anything in your life that you could change right now, what would it be?"

Without missing a beat, she said, "Not a thing."

I couldn't believe it. "You mean you can't think of anything you would change about your situation?" I observed her worn face with skin that was breaking down.

"No, not really."

I hadn't even asked her for advice, yet her simple words

spoke volumes. My eyes watered. My heart bowed low.

At night, we'd sing a simple song while I stood by her hospital bed. At seven years old when I was away from my mommy at camp, night could be pretty scary, so as I sang this song. I trusted in the fact that I had heavenly guards:

"All night, all day, angels watching over me, my Lord, all night, all day, angels watching over me."

Mom sang in her raspy bass-like voice that used to be a piercing soprano. I held her paper-thin hands and wondered if angels watched over my mama. My faith at seven may have been stronger than it was in my fifties.

My godly mother's slow death taxed my faith in a loving God. I held on, but my faith-cord seemed to be growing thin. It's a good thing I didn't have to do the hanging on. Christ did it for me.

Another faith challenge that presented itself was money. It kept shrinking. Sure, we had enough to live on thanks to Mom, but the farm seemed to be depleting our savings. I thought we'd make a bundle, when in fact, we were spending a bundle and working a bunch.

Our marriage began to suffer. I mean, Tom is an X and I am a Y. He is from Mars and I am from Venus, and living together, working together, and making every single tiny decision together made us grouchy.

We were exhausted and needed a break.

GROWING IN CHRIST

Hope is priceless, isn't it? When you lose hope, the pit of despair is waiting to swallow you up. At least, it was me for me.

Here's the problem. I shouldn't have lost hope. I fell into despair for two reasons—failing to give thanks in all things, and not believing Him. I didn't trust Him with my circumstances, and I questioned His goodness without really realizing it.

Several characters in the Bible suffered with despair but especially those in the psalms. Psalm 42 talks about a man who used to go to worship but for some reason was no longer able to.

"As the deer longs for streams of water,
so I long for you, O God.
I thirst for God, the living God.
When can I go and stand before him?
Day and night I have only tears for food,
while my enemies continually taunt me, saying,
'Where is this God of yours?'
My heart is breaking
as I remember how it used to be:
I walked among the crowds of worshipers,
leading a great procession to the house of God,
singing for joy and giving thanks
amid the sound of a great celebration!
Why am I discouraged?
Why is my heart so sad?" (NLT)

That is how I felt. Disconnected. Without hope. In the pit of despair. Several times a day I got on my knees and cried out to God. I didn't care if I lived. I sang the song "I Need You, Oh I Need You" over and over again.

Praise God, he lifted me out of that pit. While there, I went from despair to dependence.

As followers of Christ, we have the greatest gift and the most hope of anyone. Eternal life with Jesus! I don't know all the details yet, but I can't wait to get there.

Have you lost hope? I have two words for you…hold on. Hold on to God's character and His Word and His people.

Psalm 40:1–3 says this,

> *"I waited patiently for the LORD to help me,*
> *and he turned to me and heard my cry.*
> *He lifted me out of the pit of despair,*
> *out of the mud and the mire.*
> *He set my feet on solid ground*
> *and steadied me as I walked along.*
> *He has given me a new song to sing,*
> *a hymn of praise to our God.*
> *Many will see what he has done and be amazed.*
> *They will put their trust in the LORD."*

How about you? What are your fears? Where is your hope? If you haven't trusted Christ alone for salvation, why don't you start there?

Chapter 10

INVESTING IN HEAVEN

"You have eternity to enjoy the honeymoon, but only a short time to prepare for the wedding." – Woodard Kroll

GOOD NEWS AND GREAT FRIENDS

We received a call from our friends in Florida. "Pauline, Michael and I need to spend some of our vacation points and we booked a place in Ormond Beach. You want to meet us there?" Diane asked.

Sure, I'd been in a wheelchair to Paris the summer before and hadn't planned more time off. I couldn't imagine that we could since not only were we leaving the farm, we also had to find someone to care for Mom. But the details fell into place, and we met our friends at Ormond Beach.

I searched the Internet on the way there since we'd never heard of it. "Tom, it says the city is a great quiet place for middle-aged couples."

"Sounds like a great fit."

Our friends hovered over the balcony in the northeastern Florida resort town. "We're in luck," Michael smirked, "they have shuffleboard."

My heart soared at the site of them. I felt as if I were in a desert and found an oasis marked friends.

We walked the beach and ate at a local spot that served "Sticky Burgers." The local delicacy combined hamburger, peanut butter, bacon, and cheese on a bun. We munched on it and watched college football.

The next day, my other friends made the three-hour trek from Clearwater to see us. We squeezed into the small condo, talked, laughed, snacked, and prayed. These were the same people who sat with us on our last night in Florida. Now the Lord saw fit to put us together for a day—just because.

I missed friends like these in North Carolina. But these friendships took years to form. Like a tree, they were watered and fertilized and even pruned. Because of this, our friendship had deep roots and could withstand a storm or even neglect.

Isn't life like that? Mine was. The Lord was fertilizing and pruning me to help me grow. It's both hard and good. And necessary. And He gives good gifts. Gifts like great friends.

Traveling home with a smile on my face, I looked forward to 2016.

AN UNEXPECTED ANSWER TO PRAYER

"Are you ready, Pauline?" We'd decided to go to town for errands and to pick up a few small Christmas gifts. In October, Tom had began to work at a local sign company to supplement the income. I still couldn't work, but enjoyed getting out, even though my mind never really stopped thinking about Mom and her care.

"Let me just pull on my boots," I said.

"Pauline," the caregiver said loudly. I smiled as I thought of her leaning over Mom's bed since Mom and I share the same name.

"Pauline," she said louder.

"You mean me?"

"Yes! Come, now!"

I raced into Mom's room. The caregiver had her fingers in Mom's mouth, speaking calmly to her. I searched Mom's face. It was a combination of fear and panic. As I watched, her eyes glazed over.

"Help me get your mother up, she may be choking! Or having a stroke! We've got to get the food out of her mouth."

Mom had a vacant far-away look in her eyes. I grabbed her on one side while Tonya said, "One, two, three, pull!" Nothing. She slapped her hard on the back. Still no response.

"We need to get behind her and pull up!" Tonya said. Tom rushed in. "Tom, get behind Pauline on the bed and pull up," she ordered. Tom climbed behind Mom on the hospital bed and yanked. No response. Her frail body flopped forward like a ragdoll. Mom's lips turned blue. I noticed her fingernails were, too.

We continued to beat on her back.

"I can't feel her pulse anymore. I think she's seizing. Let's put her on her left side!" Tonya shouted.

My mind raced to the hospice forms we had filled out about Mom's last wishes. "Tom, put in a Christmas CD." I pulled up a chair alongside Mom's bed and stroked her hand.

This is it, after all these years, this is it. She was unresponsive. Still I spoke soothingly to her, telling her of our love for her as "O Come All Ye Faithful" played softly in the background. I held both of her hands in mine, looked at my mother's lifeless body and thought, I'm not ready for her to go.

That thought shocked me. After all this time and all my responsibility, all the times I wondered and dreamed of what my life would be like without caregiving responsibilities, I didn't want to lose Mom. I couldn't believe it.

She lay on her side, eyes glossy and lifeless. Without thinking, I cried out to God. "No! No, please!" I'm not even sure exactly what I said, I just knew I was desperate.

Silence.

Suddenly, Mom took a sharp intake of breath. Her eyes flitted. "Mom! Mom!"

Slowly she looked toward me. I continued to sob while Tonya cleaned Mom off and got her comfortable.

That day was a turning point for me—a surprising answer to prayer. You see, I'd been praying to "finish well" with Mom, but my heart wasn't in it. I prayed to be a servant in whatever situation the Lord put me, but I remained discontented and depressed.

After that day when I looked at my mother, I no longer saw a duty, but a privilege. The Lord saw fit to give me more time with her on this earth. And I was glad.

A NEW KIND OF CHRISTMAS

I'm not saying my mental state was cured, but it was much better. My spiritual state, too. I spent more time in God's Word, and made an appointment with my doctor to get some medicine.

All of it helped.

Having my daughter close helped. For my own sanity and enjoyment, I traveled the two hours to Chapel Hill to visit, clean, and care for my grandson almost every week.

Having my son in Florida still made me sad. He and his wife were separated and Micah spent the holidays alone—except for his beastly German Shepherd, Kratos. That hurt my mama heart for sure.

Sarah suggested we see him. "Mom, I get to see you a lot, but Micah might need his mom right now. Let's go see him." That idea came from heaven. My daughter, son-in-law, grandson, and I loaded a plane bound for Clearwater for a weekend trip. I'd stay with friends while the Healys would stay with Sarah's friend. But our main mission remained—be there for Micah.

Seeing him made my heart feel better. He met Silas for the first time and it was love at first sight. We ate out and visited friends. One evening our family had a serious talk in Micah's apartment.

"Micah, I think it might be good for you to get away from here and near family," I suggested. There are several hospitals around where you could work, and when you needed help, we would be there for you."

"You could always look at Atlanta, too, Micah," Sarah added. He promised to think about it.

We left a few days before Christmas without him, but I cannot describe to you what a burden was lifted just to see my son.

David and Sarah and Silas joined us for Christmas a few days later. We plunked Mom down into the chair by the fire, read the Christmas story, and sang "Happy Birthday" to Jesus.

Only a few gifts adorned the tree—but for the first time in months, I felt hope.

SLOWING DOWN AND SAVORING TIME

Snow piled up on the front porch railing. Mom and I bundled up on the warm porch that faced south. Mom listed to the left in her wheelchair while I sat next to her in a rocker. The silence could be felt, and we embraced it. Tom taught Sunday school in town and the caregiver had the day off. Just Mom and me and quiet and sun shining on our faces and into our heart.

Peace.

I glanced at Mom's creased face as she rested in the moment. Soon, a bird flitted onto the railing. Our wily cat Bree planned his attack. I foiled it by picking him up, turning him upside down and petting him. He purred contentedly, then hopped down and onto Mom's lap.

I think winter gets a bad rap. For over thirty years I lived in Florida where the forecast almost always remained the same, hot and humid with an afternoon thunderstorm. Until moving to North Carolina, I hadn't realized how much I'd missed the seasons. The change. The wonder.

Winter is a time to slow down and rest. A time to evaluate and plan. And a time to meditate. Maybe that is why most people don't love it—it gives them too much time to think.

We stared out onto the snow-covered pasture with snippets of red clay peeking through. Gazing through the trees, we could see way into the woods and across into the other field with two green tobacco barns adorning the horizon.

"Mom, see the cardinal," I pointed out. She looked and hardly saw but smiled anyway. "How are you doing today, Mom?"

"Good," she said and closed her eyes again. When I looked at my mother's face, I didn't see inconvenience anymore, but I saw wisdom and contentment and love and faithfulness. Caregiving had become a joy—still difficult, but difficulty laced with faith, hope, and love.

I wondered how long she would be with us. I held her hand each evening, prayed with her and sang. And she was grateful.

So was I.

The evenings were filled with reruns of live fires in the woodstove. Mom slumped in our big chair while Tom and I lounged on the couch. It was amazing how different the fires looked each evening and how enjoyable they were. I wasn't sure Mom could see the flames, but she felt the warmth and was content.

She'd been through ninety-five winters. Winter times in her life like when my father lost both legs to diabetes. She faced that winter squarely and not only lived through it, but exemplified to me how a godly woman faces trials. She also faced a winter in her life when I rebelled, told them I didn't believe what they did, and walked away from their faith. She remained faithful, though.

Every once in a while, she'd still say something to me like, "I wish I could help. I hate to see you work so hard."

And I almost cried. I knew my work had been mediocre and faithless. But what I said was, "Mom, you shouldn't worry about that. It's a privilege to serve you."

And I meant it.

LOADING PIGS

All winter I'd fed chickens, dogs, cats, and pigs. One of the four pigs had already gone to market the previous fall. It fell on me to care for the other three, and I didn't like them. They scared me. Each day when I approached their pen, they drooled and snorted and had a rather sinister look. They upset their food trough every day, but I refused to enter their domain, choosing instead to throw the food over to their pig space. What can I say, I didn't want to be human bacon. We decided to process all three.

The trouble would be getting them to agree to load onto the trailer, so we YouTubed it. A happy man parked his trailer behind the pigs, put feed into his trailer, and called them. "Here, piggy, piggy, piggy!" he shouted. They obliged the cheery farmer by trotting into the trailer, piggy smiles on their filthy faces like they had tickets to the Super Bowl.

"It's easy, Tom. We just borrow Alvin's trailer and get them to go in with food."

Our friend brought his trailer over and parked it next to the pigs. "I'll pick them up in a few days," he said.

The next cold, snowy February morning arrived. Tom packed feed into a white bucket and traipsed out to the pigpen. A few hours later, he returned. "I tried everything, Pauline.

They get close, but won't get in. The really big one won't even get close. We need to think of some food they can't resist."

"How about bacon?" I asked.

Tom frowned. We ended up with a combination of yellow rice, food scraps, and sausage grease from their predecessor. "I think I need your help."

I stood in the trailer holding a bucket of enticing food scraps. I borrowed the cheery farmer's words. "Here piggy, piggy, piggy," I called innocently. No response. Then a few snorts and suspicious squinty eyes.

"Let them smell it, Pauline."

Moving to the edge of the trailer, I waved the delicacies around, wafting them toward the animals as I carefully stepped backwards. "Come on, Miss Piggy, this is fine dining!"

Truthfully, I felt guilty. Passages from the book of Proverbs came to mind about following an evil woman leading to death. But then I remembered the sausage and ham from our first piggy and my mouth watered.

"Come on up, lady! The food is great!" She inched closer, putting two hooves on the ramp.

"You're doing great, Pauline," Tom whispered. "That is the farthest she's come."

Just when the female passed the threshold of the trailer, the male jumped on the ramp, startling them both, causing their immediate evacuation.

"The cheery farmer made it look so easy," I said to Tom as we walked back to our house. "Literally, the pigs just trotted into the trailer. I think they must have been pig actors," I offered.

A few days later, all three loaded and our friend took them to market. A few weeks later we traveled to the meat processing plant and stuffed our mini-van with frozen pork. And it's good.

I did feel a little guilty—but only for a second. Between our farm-fresh eggs from the ladies, deer from our property, fresh pork, and our frozen vegetables, we truly ate well.

AN EVACUATION

Despite the fact we weren't making any money with eggs, we decided to add more chickens. Ours were getting older, and we figured buying them in the spring would help us in the egg department, especially during the winter.

Again, seventy-five one-day-old chicks arrived at the post office. This time we were a bit more prepared. They lived on our big porch in the brooder we'd built for the others. When they got too big, we found an old trampoline, put it in the front yard, and surrounded it with nylon netting. When they continued to sneak out, we put our white shocker fence around the netting.

Sam watched from afar, but Barnabas seemed quite curious. When I watched him, it seemed as if he had a lustful look in his eyes. When he noticed my gaze, he looked away.

Soon, the teenage chicks began to fly out. "It's not safe out there, girls," I tried to tell them, but I didn't speak chicken. Soon we found a dead chicken in our yard. Then I noticed a few more were missing. Barnabas still had that lustful look. One day I came outside to see chicken feet sticking out of his mouth and then they slid down his throat.

Time for a chicken intervention.

We planned the move for late at night after they began to roost. But it rained and the ground was saturated. We had no choice. Taking a two-hour nap before our task, I thought we were up to it.

I noticed Tom had a bright red light shining out of his forehead. "What's on your head?" He turned to face me and the bright light shone in my face, temporarily blinding me.

"It's a red light to be able to see the birds." He looked like a wild miner/dentist. I moved on.

"So, let me get this straight—we're going to load the chickens into the coolers, drive them to the other side of our property and lock them into the new small coop we have?"

"Right. We'll keep Molly and the other birds away for a few days in the other electric fence until they get used to each other."

Tom crawled under the trampoline in the rain and handed sleeping chickens to me to put in large coolers. It went well for a while until one hen decided to wake up and inform every other bird that the sky was falling. Then we chased chickens in the dark, in the rain, with chicken poop under our feet.

After four coolers full of chickens, and two hours in the rain, we settled them next to the other ladies in the field. We trudged back to the house with filthy coolers and even filthier clothes. We stood on the back porch. "Let's strip here, Tom, and throw our clothes right in the washer."

"I'm too tired for a shower, Pauline," I noticed a grin under his bright red forehead.

"Then I guess you're sleeping outside."

My boots already had holes in them, so I threw both my boots and my socks away.

By the way, remember I told you we ordered seventy-five? When we transferred them to the field, there were fifty-six left.

I guess dogs have to eat, too.

Maybe we needed an evacuation plan for Barnabas.

SAYING GOODBYE

About the third week of March I propped Mom up in the big leather chair in front of a hearty fire. Pulling out the hymnbook, I asked her what she wanted to sing.

"You choose, Pauline."

I opened it up and sang a variety of old favorites. Mom sang along when she remembered the words and it made me smile. The last hymn I chose was "When We All Get to Heaven." Mom joined me on the chorus.

"When we all get to heaven, what a day of rejoicing that will be. When we all see Jesus we'll sing and shout the victory!"

She sang robustly, not in her usual raspy, old-person voice, but with her strong and steady younger woman voice in the same octave as me. She threw back her head and closed her eyes.

After we finished, I said, "That will be great, Mom, won't it? To be in heaven one day?"

She smiled slightly, looked me straight in the eyes and said, "That will be great."

That night, when I went to bed, I told the Lord if He wanted to take my mama to be with Him that night, it was all right with me. But He decided to wait a few more days.

It had been a rough few days. The Friday before while putting Mom to bed I noticed she felt warm so I took her temperature. It read 102.5. Mom and I hardly ever run fevers. Our normal body temperature is low—about 97 degrees. When I saw the reading, I phoned hospice.

The weekend nurse arrived shortly after 9 p.m. "She may just have a virus; we'll have to wait and see. Just keep her comfortable and give her Tylenol regularly for the fever."

Mom was coherent, just weak. I kept an eye on her and called my sisters the next day. "Mom is pretty sick. I don't know what she has but she's running a high fever," I told them. Neither could come and we didn't feel it was necessary. Paula was just with us, and we were all together for Mom's ninety-fifth birthday.

The next night I called the nurse again. And I called the next day—which is unusual since I had only called hospice and asked them to come to our house about three times in sixteen months.

But by Monday, her fever dropped a little and she ate more.

So that Tuesday night I insisted on dinner out with my husband. In between sobs, I said, "I think we should talk about end-of-life issues." I blew my nose and wiped my eyes. "Mom's better, but when she does get ready to go to heaven, I don't want anyone else there except you and me."

I shifted in my chair, avoiding the eyes of other customers. "Because you and I have been at this a long time. We've been a team. I don't want family, friends, caregivers, hospice workers…anyone! I want us to finish well," I sobbed.

"Okay, Pauline. It's okay." He patted my arm.

Our plan that night was to sneak through the front door into our bedroom, while the caregiver prepared Mom for bed. We'd hang out together for the rest of the evening. But as soon as I walked through the front door with Tom, my mother began to groan. She'd never done that before.

I entered her room and Tonya said, "She just started that when you came in. I've been feeding her some applesauce and she's eaten a lot."

"Why don't you go home, Tonya? We've got this."

Mom groaned. I spoke softly to her and took her hand as Tonya left. I thought she was in pain and gave her some medicine. I put in another call to hospice. The nurse was on her way.

Tom came in as *NCIS* played in the background. We watched TV, but Mom wouldn't stop groaning. I took her hand and tried talking to her. Soon, her breathing shifted to hard panting. I tried reading Scripture to her, but nothing helped. Finally, it dawned on me that she was dying.

I threw my arms around the side of her while she breathed hard. "Mom, I just want you to know that we love you so much. And you've been a great mom." Her panting grew stronger and rougher as my sobs increased. Tom took her other hand. "And your life has made a difference in our lives and many other peoples' lives, too." I hugged her so tight as I wept and said, "I love you, Mom. I love you, Mom."

Her breathing stopped mid-breath.

Silence.

Tom looked at me and said, "You finished well, Pauline, you finished well."

A DIFFERENT TIME

Within the hour, the hospice nurse had come and the funeral home took Mom's body away.

And then Tom and I were alone in our new house for the first time ever. It seemed unnatural and strange. One minute, my mother lay in my arms—the next minute, she was gone. Silently, we left Mom's room and sat on the couch. The clock read about eleven p.m. I'd already called my sisters and my children. All the other arrangements could wait until tomorrow.

We held hands in the silence, and then we prayed. That night, Tom held me close as I thought about the day, the month, the year, my parents, and my life.

We woke up the next morning to an empty house. Reverently, I entered Mom's room. Her bed lay empty with the exception of a sheet. I sat in the chair and listened. No TV, no NCIS. That time of my life had passed along with Mom.

Soon, I made all the necessary phone calls. My sisters and I spoke on the phone and distributed duties. I got off easy. A few phone calls and Tom and I would be on our way to Florida within the week for Mom's funeral.

We received several calls from people from my church along with visits and meals. All were appreciated. I didn't post anything on social media. Frankly, I didn't want to announce it. I just wanted to rest and think.

Several months earlier, Tom told me that when Mom died, I should take two weeks off and visit friends. Trouble was, one friend had a scheduled trip to Disney, the other to Israel. The plan was for us to attend the funeral and Tom to fly home the next day. I would only stay a few days. Sarah and Silas stayed, too, which gave us a chance to visit with Micah.

My father's funeral had been one of the happiest funerals I'd ever been to. Mom's was no different. We celebrated family, friends, but especially we celebrated our hope in Jesus to not only see her again, but to see our Savior—to sit on His big heavenly porch and talk for hours—to worship fully and see clearly—to have the hope that followers of Christ share because of the death and resurrection of our Lord.

We had a grand time.

But then time took over our lives and everyone returned home. When I arrived at the Charlotte airport, Tom picked me up.

"How's work going?" I asked.

He made a funny face. "I didn't want to tell you this right away, but today I got laid off."

I didn't care. "It's a God thing, Tom. Don't worry. We need some time alone."

And we did. The next day, I had a fever of 102 and stayed down for a week while my husband cared for me. Tom got an interview the following Monday and began a new job for a different sign company the Monday after.

Our new different life had begun. Now what? I wondered.

GROWING IN CHRIST

Once upon a time when newspapers were delivered to my door daily, I used to read the obituaries. Don't laugh. The thought of condensing a person's entire life in a few paragraphs intrigued me. Of course, some were long and extensive, while others announced the deceased's death in a sentence or two.

I often wondered about those people. No relatives listed, no service, just a notice of death. What was their life like? Where was their family? Did their life make a difference?

And then I ask myself that last question. Will my life make a difference? Don't get me wrong. I don't care if I'm ever famous. The chances of that are slim to none. What I ask myself is, will the fact that I lived in this world make a lasting difference—an eternal difference?

One thing is true, we are all going to die. And knowing that should affect the way we live, right? I call it my Investing in Heaven Stock. In Matthew 6:19–20 Jesus said this, "Don't store up treasures here on earth, where moths eat them and rust destroys them, and where thieves break in and steal. Store your treasures in heaven, where moths and rust cannot destroy, and thieves do not break in and steal" (NLT).

My mom's life made a difference, so did my dad's. The desire of my heart is that when I am promoted to glory, others will have seen Christ in me.

What about you, my friend? Have you considered the fact that one day your life on this planet will end?

Sometimes I find myself spending days worrying about what people think or deciding on the color of a rug when I should be investing in heaven. Psalm 90:12 says, "So teach us to number our days, That we may present to You a heart of wisdom."

Considering those hard questions will help you live your life now. Taking stock of your life in the light of eternity is wise.

You've heard the phrase You can't take it with you. That is true, but you can leave something behind.

A legacy.

Epilogue

THE SHEPHERD AND HIS SHEEP

"He will feed his flock like a shepherd. He will carry the lambs in his arms, holding them close to his heart. He will gently lead the mother sheep with their young." Isaiah 40:11 NLT

SURPRISED

Pauline! Our ewe is having a lamb!"

I had trouble hearing since phone reception wasn't great in our church. It was a Wednesday night, and a group of us practiced the music for the following Sunday.

"I'm sorry, our what is having a what?" I shouted.

"Our sheep is having a lamb right now! I can see the hooves!"

Jumping up and down on the stage I yelled, "We're having lambs! We're having baby lambs!"

I rushed home. As a baby lamb got unsteadily to its feet and began to nurse, we watched from over the fence Tom had spent months building. Stunning. Miraculous. Beautiful.

Within six weeks our tiny flock of hair sheep went from five to eleven. Two sets of twins and two individual lambs. Here's the rub…we didn't even know they were pregnant.

Rookies.

The first lamb births took place in March of 2018. I am finishing this last section of Growing in Christ from the Ground Up in March of 2019. As of yesterday, we have twenty sheep, ten new lambs, and ten older sheep. I didn't know the Lord would see fit to make us shepherds.

But we are.

A lot has changed in the three years since Mom went to heaven in March of 2016. Let me help you catch up.

After she died, I stared at the walls and sat in my living room for six months. Normally, I love to be around people but after fourteen years of caregiving for my parents, raising a family, moving to a new state, leaving all of my friends and church family, and starting a farm...let's just say exhausted didn't begin to cover how I felt.

I enjoyed the solitude, the stillness of the farm. I had a lot of thinking and remembering and grieving to do.

Tom continued to work at a sign company and for that first year he worked about sixty hours a week. On the one day he had off, he put up fencing for our newly cleared pasture.

After the first six months, I began to apply for jobs. I had a few interviews for jobs I'm glad I did not get. Being out of the workforce for over a decade and not in a professional position for longer put me at a distinct disadvantage.

Finally, I applied to be a case manager in a rural county next to ours. I got the job. You see, I graduated from college with a Bachelor of Social Work when phones still hung on the wall. And even though I've done a lot of social working in my life—including fourteen years of caregiving, I'd never actually been a social worker.

I went into the job thinking I knew a lot. After a few months, my arrogant self realized the job entailed more than just talking to people, checking on them, and caring for them. There were guidelines, deadlines, and a chain of command. I had to remember a lot and oversee clients' budgets. There were daysheets to fill out, time sheets to manage, and a copy machine that could probably run my entire house. Those aren't exactly my strengths.

I was and am the dumbest social worker on my hall. I am also the oldest. I'm not proud of either, but they are the truth. And I can handle the truth.

By the way, we failed at farming. That surprised me. It didn't surprise anyone else. Both Tom and I worked incredibly hard and unbelievably long hours and thought we could survive on farming income. But the money wasn't enough. In fact, it wasn't even a little. Each month, we continued to lose money until now when we just grow enough vegetables for ourselves and to share. Our acre of asparagus lies dormant and one day we may be able to revive it, but not now.

I have exactly seventeen hens and one rooster. They are now in a chicken fence next to my house. This morning when I looked out, I noticed chickens wandering around and outside of our yard. Outside the fence. I have told them again and again that it is not better outside the fence, but like I mentioned before, I don't speak chicken.

Turns out, the electric fence has no charge, and because of the rain, the fence fell down in spots, so the ladies just wandered out. I put my boots on and took care of the problem. Then I put on grown-up clothes and makeup and got ready for work.

In fact, both Tom and I go off to work Monday through Friday, and each put in about forty hours our per week in our perspective careers. And we get paid. Amazing.

Then comes the weekend. Most of you have enjoyed weekends for years, but for Tom and me, it's a new experience. Before we moved to the farm, our fishing business was year-round and any day that we had a charter scheduled and the weather was good became a work day. We could never count on weekends until Tom decided to take off most Sundays the last five years we lived in Florida.

In fact, I used to tell my kids, I have good news and bad news. The good news is your dad is off work. The bad news is your dad is off work.

Now we come home on Friday nights and do the weekend dance. After we celebrate with a fine meal and watch a little baseball, we fall into bed between eight and nine.

We rise at about six a.m., drink coffee, watch the sunrise, and enjoy the fact that we don't have to work. At about nine-ish, we dress in work clothes and get busy on Peeled Poplar Farm. We work on the farm all day Saturday and some on Sunday.

And we love it.

ANSWERS TO PRAYERS

A few years before we moved, I wrote specific, long-term prayer requests. I use an index card system that I learned from a book titled *A Praying Life* by Paul Miller. I highly recommend that book. It has changed my life.

On one card I made several requests specific to me. I asked the Lord to make my husband known in the gates—not me (Proverbs 31:23). I've always been such a loud-mouth that Tom often drifted into the background. My desire was for that to change.

Attending our new church answered that prayer. Tom began to teach a Sunday school class and because of Mom's condition, often I remained home. He became involved in running the sound equipment and even became a deacon. I am thankful for that.

On that same card I asked Jesus to help repair the relationship with our son. Those last several years in Florida were tough on all of us. When we moved away there was a definite rift, especially between Tom and Micah. A few years ago, Micah moved about four miles up the road from us. That was a God thing. He is a city boy and a Florida boy through and through. But because of extremely difficult circumstances, he really had no choice.

He lives on a local man's land in a small two-bedroom house. There is a large pond across the street and livestock around him. One morning, shortly after he arrived in North Carolina, he sent me a text that read, Cow in the middle of my driveway. Made me laugh.

Gradually, our relationship is improving. The circumstances of his move here were not at all what I would have chosen, but God is sovereign, and He heard my prayer.

Another request was the same request Moses made in Exodus 33. I asked that I would know the Lord, that He would go with me, and that I would see His glory. Lately, I have realized how He answers that prayer for all believers. As we pray and read His Word, we get to know Him.

When we are His children, His Spirit resides within us and goes with us. The Spirit teaches, comforts, convicts, encouragers, and prays for us. Moses did not have Jesus in him—as believers, we do. In John 15 Jesus promised the Comforter would come.

I'm glad.

I see His glory in my answered prayers. Some very difficult answers but sifted through the hands of a loving God who has my best in mind when He deals with me and my family.

The last request on that card was for the Lord to increase my faith. I mentioned earlier that my conception of the amount of faith I had was mountainous when in reality it was hardly visible.

The whole situation of being taken out of my comfort zone

was a big reminder of my utter dependence on God. He has rubbed off some rough edges of pride and self-sufficiency. And there are still many more of those edges.

I think the biggest change in my life was a deeper understanding of the gospel. That should surprise you. I grew up in the church, was saved in college, baptized, taught classes, I've even written a Bible study.

Yet, I am just beginning to catch a glimpse of the good news. For years I have said it is grace alone by faith alone through Christ alone, but didn't comprehend the simplicity. I guess I thought God needed me and my works counted somehow in His heavenly scheme. I was one of God's VIPs. Pitiful.

Through utter helplessness and much-needed humiliation I have begun to understand both how undeserving I am and how loved I am by God. He holds me fast. It is not about me, but about Him. He did not create me to be happy, but holy. And curiously, that makes me happy.

GROWING IN CHRIST

Remember how the name Peeled Poplar Farm came from the book of Genesis? Jacob stripped poplar branches and placed them near the watering source to increase his herd of sheep and goats.

God has given us a flock and now we are shepherds. We are just learning about sheep. In our first batch of lambs, one mother would not nurse her baby. So, we did—Little Orphan Annie.

In our most recent births, there have been some deaths. One had to be killed because she had a bad leg and its mother had rejected her. This almost killed Tom. One froze. Two were born dead. And a weak one died last night. We are down to nineteen.

Here is what we have learned so far.

Sheep have no defenses. One time, as I approached a new

mother, she looked me square in the eye and stomped her foot. That is all she could do to protect her lamb. The only other protection is for them to flee.

When our first batch of sheep were older, I would let my house dogs into the pasture to play with Molly, our guard dog. They'd run and get tired and then I would bring them home. One day I left them longer than usual. When I got to the pasture, I noticed two of the sheep were standing in the pond as Barnabas ran around them barking furiously.

And speaking of furious, Tom waded into the water and pulled our drenched sheep out. Let's just say I slept on the couch that night. My point is, sheep run. That is what they do. They need a good shepherd to protect them. I failed Shepherding 101 that day.

They will also wander; some wool sheep fall over and cannot get back up. It is called being cast. In W. Phillip Keller's book *A Shepherd Looks at Psalm 23*, he describes a sheep as being cast down. It is life-threatening, and the shepherd needs to be constantly protecting and caring for their sheep. He will actually need to turn them over to save their lives.

However, the trait that stands out most to me with the little lambs is their innocence. They have no way to defend themselves, are completely dependent on their ewes, and are incredibly docile.

A few weeks after we lost some lambs and Tom had to put one out of its misery, I listened to a message in church about the Passover Lamb. I could not stop weeping.

Finally, I had a real-life picture of what I'd read in the Bible for years. When God was to deliver the people of Israel from the Egyptians, he required all of the Israelites to take in a small lamb that would live with them for a few weeks. At the end of that time, they would kill the innocent lamb in order for the

Angel of God to "pass over" the sins of the people.

Sin had to be covered. That is what the lamb's blood did for the Israelites.

I pictured the little lambs we own. Then I remembered the Passover Lamb in Isaiah 53:1–7.

"Who has believed our message?
To whom has the LORD revealed his powerful arm?
My servant grew up in the LORD's presence like a tender green shoot, like a root in dry ground.
There was nothing beautiful or majestic about his appearance, nothing to attract us to him.
He was despised and rejected—a man of sorrows, acquainted with deepest grief.
We turned our backs on him and looked the other way.
He was despised, and we did not care.
Yet it was our weaknesses he carried;
it was our sorrows that weighed him down.
And we thought his troubles were a punishment from God, a punishment for his own sins!
But he was pierced for our rebellion, crushed for our sins.
He was beaten so we could be whole.
He was whipped so we could be healed.
All of us, like sheep, have strayed away.
We have left God's paths to follow our own.
Yet the LORD laid on him the sins of us all.
He was oppressed and treated harshly,
yet he never said a word.
He was led like a lamb to the slaughter.
And as a sheep is silent before the shearers,
he did not open his mouth" (NLT).

That is the gospel. Jesus, the innocent Son of God, was led to a Roman cross to die a cruel death for my sin. For your sin.

That is where this journey has led me. I hope it is where this journey has led you whether you live in a city or in the suburbs. Whether you sit at a desk or work on a farm. I pray that you are growing in Christ. It is a life-long process on this earth. But one day we will see the Passover Lamb.

The Passover Lamb is calling. Will you answer His call?

About the Author

Formerly from Florida, Pauline Hylton now lives with her husband, Tom, three dogs, ten chickens, a cat, two pigs, and twenty-one sheep on a sixty-six-acre tobacco farm Tom inherited in Mount Airy, North Carolina. They've tried farming, but it's not as easy as it looks and pays almost nothing. So now they each work a day job and farm on the weekends.

Her articles appear monthly on CBN.com. Her work has also appeared in *USA Today, Chicken Soup for the Soul, Christianity Today,* the *Tampa Bay Times*, and several other publications. Pauline loves her Lord, her family, and dark chocolate. (Not necessarily in that order.)

PaulineHylton.com
Facebook.com/PaulineHyltonAuthor
Twitter.com/seepaulinewrite

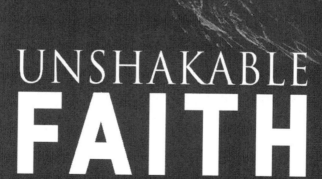

UNSHAKABLE
FAITH

Living Strong in the Kingdom of God

More great books from...
CROSSRIVERMEDIA.COM

ABBA'S PROMISE
Debra L. Butterfield

When trouble strikes, we can find ourselves doubting God's Word. But from our smallest to our biggest need, Abba Father promised to provide. The testimony of how God works in our lives is a powerful weapon against our doubts. In *Abba's Promise*, you'll find thirty-three personal stories of God's provision. Discover how God used purple socks, a steel pipe, and a corn maze to answer prayers. Start your day with a dose of faith. These true stories will cure your fear and doubts.

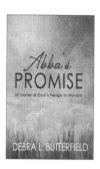

THE BENEFIT PACKAGE
Tamara Clymer

Love, redemption, mercy, provision, revelation and healing… In Psalm 103, David listed just a few of the good things God did for him. His list gives us plenty to be thankful for during tough times. No matter your circumstances or background, God is always full of compassion, generous with His mercy, unfailing in His love and powerful in healing. When circumstances overwhelm you — unwrap His *Benefit Package* and rediscover God's goodness.

THE GRACE IMPACT
Nancy Kay Grace

The promise of grace pulses throughout Scripture. Chapter after chapter, the Bible shows a loving heavenly Father lavishing His grace on us through His son. In her book, *The Grace Impact*, author Nancy Kay Grace gives us a closer glimpse at God's character. His grace covers every detail of life, not just the good things, but the difficult, sad and complicated things. That knowledge can give us the ability to walk confidently through life knowing God is with us every step of the way.

Unbeaten

How biblical heroes rose above
their pain... and you can too.

Available in bookstores and from online retailers.

CrossRiver Media
www.crossrivermedia.com

If you enjoyed this book, will you consider sharing it with others?

- Please mention the book on Facebook, Twitter, Pinterest, or your blog.

- Recommend this book to your small group, book club, and workplace.

- Head over to Facebook.com/CrossRiverMedia, 'Like' the page and post a comment as to what you enjoyed the most.

- Pick up a copy for someone you know who would be challenged or encouraged by this message.

- Write a review on Amazon.com, BN.com, or Goodreads.com.

- To learn about our latest releases, subscribe to our newsletter at www.CrossRiverMedia.com.

Made in the USA
Columbia, SC
17 August 2021